THE SCREAM OF THE WHISTLE

A MESSAGE FROM CHICKEN HOUSE

I love a spooky story – and it doesn't get much spookier than an abandoned railway station with a disastrous and deadly past! Join Ruby as she explores the mysterious *Green Lady*, a steam locomotive where ghostly memories are her travelling companions. But will you arrive at the final destination? All aboard for an eerie ride!

BARRY CUNNINGHAM
Publisher
Chicken House

THE SCREAM OF THE WHISTLE

Emily Randall-Jones

2 Palmer Street, Frome, Somerset BA11 1DS
www.chickenhousebooks.com

First published in the UK in 2025
Chicken House
2 Palmer Street
Frome, Somerset BA11 1DS
United Kingdom
www.chickenhousebooks.com

Chicken House/Scholastic Ireland, 89E Lagan Road, Dublin Industrial Estate,
Glasnevin, Dublin D11 HP5F, Republic of Ireland

Text © Emily Randall-Jones 2025
Illustration © Micaela Alcaino 2025

The moral rights of the author and illustrator have been asserted.

All rights reserved.
No part of this publication may be reproduced, transmitted, downloaded,
decompiled, reverse engineered, used to train any artificial intelligence
technologies, or stored in or introduced into any information storage and
retrieval system, in any form or by any means, whether electronic or mechanical,
now known or hereafter invented, without the express written permission
of the publisher. Subject to EU law the publisher expressly reserves this
work from the text and data mining exception.

This book is a work of fiction. Names, characters, businesses, organizations,
places, events and incidents are either the product of the author's imagination
or used in a fictitious manner. Any resemblance to actual persons, living or
dead, events or locales is purely coincidental.

For safety or quality concerns:
UK: www.chickenhousebooks.com/productinformation
EU: www.scholastic.ie/productinformation

Cover design by Micaela Alcaino
Typeset by Dorchester Typesetting Group Ltd
Printed in the UK by Clays, Elcograf S.p.A

1 3 5 7 9 10 8 6 4 2

A CIP catalogue record for this book is available from the British Library.

PB ISBN 978-1-915947-14-7
eISBN 978-1-917171-17-5

For Mum and Dad.
Thank you for the stories, the steam trains,
the magic honeypots and the treasure hunts.
Love you always x

ONE

When they pulled into Melbridge, Ru's bravery almost crumbled to dust.

It was even worse than she'd remembered.

They'd only been once before, but she didn't like it when she was six and she *definitely* didn't like it now she was twelve. Just as then, thirteen identical houses stood locked together in a row, weather-beaten and broken. Ghosts of the long-dead railway village, made from stone as grey as storm clouds. Most of them seemed too rotten to be upright, let alone lived in.

'Good job Gram normally comes to ours,' she muttered to her brother as they got out of the car. He ignored her.

'You going in, folks?' Mum staggered past, crumpled under the weight of their cat, Grizabella. 'Or are you planning on sleeping out here?'

Maybe I'd prefer it, Ru thought. But she smiled with her teeth and gave two thumbs up. 'In a minute. Just . . . taking it in.'

'Suit yourself. And remember not to ask about Gram's hippy stuff. It makes her go bizarre.'

Bizarre was an understatement for this whole place. There was a strange taste in the air – bitter and acrid, like charred hair. Little Hampton this definitely wasn't.

If Ru had allowed a sad thought to creep in just then, she'd be desperate to go home. Desperate for the games cupboard that stretched to the ceiling and the glass doors thrown open to their wild, overrun garden. But all that was gone now, replaced by the memory of Dad's wave wilting like a dead plant as they turned out of the drive and left him behind.

It was a good job she was staying positive.

Challenge: Shake it off, Ru. Get your head back in the game.

A defiant chin in the air, Ru followed Mum up the path into the only house lit up – Gram's cottage – making a mental note to superglue the headless gnome outside the door.

NO PLACE LIKE GNOME was carved beneath his boots.

On second thoughts, maybe she'd leave it.

Inside was a cluttered chocolate box full of knick-knacks. Incense and dried lavender, ticking clocks, battered books and saucers of garibaldi biscuits. 'Dead-fly biscuits', Mum called them. Tasted like it, too.

Gram flicked a distracted hand in the air as Ru came in. She was bent over a remote control, showing Mum how to work the TV.

'And you press the red button to turn it off, Martha. The *red button*. You got that?'

'So that's the green button, Ma?' Mum caught Ru's eye with a twinkly smirk.

'No, Martha, the red bu . . . look, let's start again.'

Ru popped a garibaldi absent-mindedly into her mouth and then swiftly spat it out again, wiping crumb mush on to a napkin.

'Ooh, and I'll just grab the WiFi password.' Gram headed up the stairs, the lace cobweb of her dress disappearing round the bend. 'It's new. Have you heard of WiFi, Martha . . . ?'

Mum's eyes followed her, before swerving

anxiously back to Ru. 'I know, I know. This is only temporary. We won't be staying here for long. We'll get a place back in Little Hampton as soon as one comes up.'

One of two places, came Ru's sneaky, stinging thought. *Homes split in half like a broken heart.* She pushed it far, far away.

'It's fine!' She beamed in the way that Mum liked. 'More than fine. It's exciting.'

Mum ruffled her hair as she went past, and Ru's red mane puffed into the shape of a fireball. 'There's my Rubes,' Mum smiled. 'Guess I'd better tell Gram the WiFi router isn't in the bathroom.'

As soon as Mum had ducked under the stair beam, a snort rumbled from the doorway. Irritation spindled, and Ru threw a withering gaze at her brother.

'Hey, that was almost a word. Does it hurt to do something other than grunt?'

With a waft of cheap aftershave and the wail of guitar music, Sam pulled his earbuds out and glared at Ru. 'Nope. Does it hurt to be so delusional?'

'Don't know what you're talking about.'

'Come on,' he whispered gently, sounding almost

human. 'You've got that Games Night glint in your eye. The house has been let. Dad's clearing out tomorrow morning. There's no going back, Rubes.'

Ru held fast, despite the wobbling of her insides.

'Shows how much you know.' She gifted him an angelic smile. 'I always win Games Night, don't I?'

'Yeah, but . . .'

'And I'll win this. It all happened too quickly at home, but now I've got time to plan. I'll get Mum and Dad back together by the end of the week.'

She didn't like the look Sam gave her. Too big-brothery.

'Whatever.' He slipped the earbuds back in and disappeared into the shadows like an annoying vampire. 'It's your funeral.'

Two

The coiled spring inside Ru tightened and pushed her to her feet. What did Sam know, anyway? He'd barely left his room in forever. Too busy writing slushy songs or painstakingly styling his frizz into curls.

Unable to keep still, she tramped around the cottage's ground floor, nosing at sage bundles, the hanging willow bent into circles and Gram's gallery of family photographs. The drizzle from outside cast a pocked, fuzzy reflection on to the frames' glass, making them look like scenes from old movies.

Ru had adored the gallery wall on her first visit. There was the old portrait of her great-great-grampy Sydney, looking miserable in engine-shed overalls. Tools and railway detritus lay in cluttered piles that surrounded him. His springy nest of hair, untamed by wax, was a mirror of Ru's; the long chin and downward turn of his mouth were the same as Sam's. Weird how long-long-dead people could look like you.

'A more chaotic, ramshackle ninny-hammer there never was,' Gram had tutted fondly. *'But what he didn't know about trains wasn't worth knowing. Such a tragedy he only drove once.'*

Next to him was a picture of Mum as a toddler, balancing on an old turntable, then young Gram in the cab of a train, wearing an effervescent grin and a too-big stationmaster's hat. She'd dreamt of becoming the Mid Wessex Line's first female driver. Too bad it never happened.

One photo Ru had loved more than any other: Mum and Dad on their wedding day, dressed up all fancy, laughing and running through a tunnel of sparklers. They shone like glow-worms, and tiny Ru had felt her own chest light up too.

But this time, the picture wasn't there.

Ru's mouth was suddenly desert-dry, the charred taste burning her throat.

Gram had taken it down? Gram thought it was over, too?

Hanging in its place was a tatty black-and-white photograph, the corners fading into white. A dozen or so grim-faced men, mostly in old railway uniforms, lined up before a towering beast of a steam train. The photo's angle made it seem that the train was going to plough them all down like skittles.

Only a few of the figures had survived what looked like a serious mould attack, and the others were speckled with black. Sydney stood in the back line, turning awkwardly from the man next to him.

There was something unnatural about his stance. Why was he turning away?

With a loud roar, a gust of wind blasted Ru sideways. The photograph rattled and toppled on to the hardwood floor with a *smash*.

Ru froze, waiting for Mum's concerned yell, the crash of feet down the stairs. But it didn't come.

Baffled, she stared at the spray of shattered glass at her feet.

What on earth?

Sam had closed the front door after himself, and all the windows were shut tight against the gloom.

Where had the wind come from?

With a quick glance around the empty room, Ru swept up the shards and guiltily nudged them underneath the nearby dresser with her toe. Maybe Gram wouldn't notice it was missing. Maybe. Hopefully.

She wouldn't think about the wedding photo. Not that it mattered anyway. Who cared if Gram thought it was over? Or Sam, or even Mum and Dad for that matter?

I'm going to fix it.

But the night didn't bring her any life-changing ideas – only a conveyor belt of unsettling dreams. Ru squirmed in her sleep, battered by images of Dad, garibaldi biscuits, clocks that ticked as loud as thunder and rows of mould-speckled men that never ended.

When she jerked awake, she was upside down on the air mattress, her matted hair sticky with sweat. Her limbs were tangled in the sleeping bag.

I'm not at home. I'm in Gram's box room.

Her heart sank to her feet.

She had no idea what time it was. Her fingers

itched for her phone, but Mum never let Ru have it in bed, and she'd left her Terry Pratchett books in the car. The piercing moonlight and Sam's wall-shaking snores meant it must be pre-5 a.m. Either super late or super early.

Her body too buzzy to stay flat, she clambered on to the messy desk in front of the bare window and sat there, hugging her knees to her chest.

The moon spread its rays like the beam of a spaceship, illuminating the old, abandoned Melbridge station in the valley behind the houses. The derelict ticket office was strangled with twisted ivy, its boarded-up windows choked with weeds. Train tracks were half-hidden beneath dead grass, and looming behind it all were broken outbuildings, with roofs caved in and stone spilt into mounds.

I don't remember this, she thought. *I wouldn't forget this.*

Something like fear clawed at her, and she leapfrogged back into bed. The neglected station didn't feel right – it was backwards and against the order of things. Nature was angrily taking back what was theirs, grasping and pulling everything down. In a few years Melbridge station would just be a lump in the ground, with no sign of how alive it had once been.

Huh.

Sounded like her family.

Three

When the sun rose to jackdaws screeching, Ru immediately felt heaps better. The swirling anxiety demons inside her thrived on darkness, but come morning she was always clear of head and ready for action.

Challenge: Get downstairs in less than thirty seconds without waking anyone. GO.

She bounded to her feet, put on her thickest socks and padded silently across the landing. A monstrous ball of brown and white fluff was spread lazily on the top stair.

'You're a liability, Grizabella,' Ru whispered, swinging her leg over the cat lump. How could a feline be so huge? 'Scooch out the way before Gram wakes up. If she trips over you, it'll be curtains.'

'Oi, I'm not that old.'

Gram's voice rang out from the lounge, and Ru jumped, trapping Grizabella's tail with her heel. The cat yowled and darted straight into Sam's room.

Ru winced. 'I'm toast. He doesn't get up before eleven at weekends.'

'Don't vex, little Firecrest,' Gram said. 'You can blame me.'

'What are you doing up so early, Gram?' Ru hopped down the remaining steps. The old woman was cross-legged on the floor in an emerald silk robe, basking in a slither of pink dawn. Dust specks glittered in the light.

'Welcoming in the sunrise, my lamb. Do you want to join me?'

'Oh . . . er . . .' Ru scrambled for the nicest way to refuse, but swiftly drew a blank. 'Sorry. I'm not very good at sitting still.'

Gram chuckled. 'No, me neither.' She climbed creakily to her feet, grunting slightly at her arthritic knees. 'Thought I should make a special effort for May Eve.'

'For what now?'

Gram blinked and gazed at Ru, as if drinking her

in. 'Follow me.' She cocked her head towards the front door.

Ru slipped on her jacket and trainers and obediently followed Gram outside on to the front step. Blackbirds gossiped from branches and the dawn's warmth tingled her skin. Melbridge was marginally less grim now the sun was out, but it was still as grey as dishwater and smelt *disgustingly* smoky. Even with all the trains long gone.

The giant tunnel they'd driven through was flanked by impenetrable stone walls that were green with algae, and blocked any view of the outside world.

Kind of like a prison gate.

The thirteen conjoined houses were deathly still, caving in on themselves.

'Can you feel the change of seasons, Ru?' Gram's Wiltshire burr was even stronger than usual. 'The Wheel of the Year turning?'

If the Wheel of the Year smells like air pollution, then yes.

'Ooh, yeah.'

'There's an earthly magic in Melbridge.' Gram gazed into the middle distance. Even in the warmth, her breath made small puffs of steam. 'It's always been its own tiny kingdom, utterly separate. And like many hamlets, we still cling to fragments of the old ways. Melbridge is as much ancient Wiltshire magic as it is railway.'

Ru nodded sagely, not sure what to say.

'Tonight is May Eve,' Gram went on. 'And tomorrow is May Day; midway between the Spring Equinox and Summer Solstice. We welcome in the warmest quarter of the year, and the boundary between worlds is at its thinnest.'

'Worlds?' Ru asked, remembering Mum's warning too late. *Don't ask about Gram's hippy stuff.*

Gram's dark eyes searched Ru's face. 'You didn't knock over that picture on my gallery wall, did you?'

A shiver swept through Ru. 'Um...'

Gram's lips twitched into a knowing smile. 'Thought not. Trickster spirits enter our world freely around May Day, little Ru. Mischief and chaos abound.'

'Oh, right. Oo-er.'

Gram guffawed and wrapped a fond arm around Ru's shoulders, enveloping her in a wave of jasmine incense. It was a welcome relief from the Melbridge stench. 'Oh, my Firecrest. You haven't changed. You've your father's brain, don't you? Logic and reason.'

The mention of Dad made Ru tighten, and the hug felt suddenly bony and awkward. 'I guess.' Static energy swirled in her feet. She needed to move, to keep the swirl from reaching her head. Without thinking, she blurted out, 'I saw the old station from the window.'

Gram looked like Ru had given her the best present in the world. 'You did? Did you like it? I'd *love* to take you round. Your mum said it wasn't your kind of thing, but she worries too much.'

'No, I . . .' Ru's gut was screaming at her. She squashed it down, because Gram looked so happy. 'I'd love to. Guess it's our history, right?'

'It certainly is.' Gram was already off, stomping towards the station in a determined curve. 'The Coles were Melbridge royalty once, Ru. Perhaps that makes you and Sam the new heirs.'

Ru laughed weakly. She wasn't a Cole. She was half-Cole, half-Darke, despite everyone trying to erase that.

Although frankly, right then she'd have given

anything to be full Darke and far, far away from the decaying corpse of Melbridge station. It was the last place she wanted to be.

Four

Ru weaved unsteadily down the hill that ran behind the cottages and on to the splintered, wonky train tracks. Spatial awareness wasn't exactly her thing, and it was hard to keep upright as she clambered after Gram.

Up close, Melbridge station was even stranger than it had been from her window. Somehow the atmosphere was different here, stale and thin and stuffy from decades of neglect. A smoke-filled grasp made its way into Ru's lungs and squeezed them tight, because it all felt so *wrong*: time-locked, as if everyone had just up and abandoned it one day, like that empty ship *Mary Celeste*. Everything left halfway finished.

MELBRIDGE was patchily painted on to a

signpost dug into a decades-dead plant border, with vines and tendrils clasping it in a chokehold. On the platform was a bench with broken slats, a large smashed clock, a rusted trolley full of decaying suitcases and some ripped bunting threads that draped from the husks of hanging flower baskets.

A ghost station.

She shouldn't be here. She should be in bed. She didn't like it.

'Why's it like this?' Ru said, unable to stop fear staining her voice. 'How come they didn't knock it down?'

'Melbridge . . .' Gram paused, avoiding Ru's eye. 'Melbridge shouldn't have ended like this. There was a . . . run of bad luck, and we never recovered. The superstitious called it a curse, but curse or not, this village was built around the station and nobody dared touch it, even after it closed. Nobody wants to. We're all connected to the railway and each other, veins to veins. If we tear out the station – its heart – we tear out our own hearts, too.'

But the heart had long gone. Melbridge was a ruined shrine to something dead. The thirteen houses were its mourners.

Gram nudged Ru towards the ticket office. 'Some of the local stations kept the steam trains going as tourist attractions, even after the old lines were shut down in the 1960s.' With a grunt she climbed on to the platform, her green silk robe trailing in black dirt. She looked like a grasshopper trapped in mud. 'We tried for a while. But we ran out of money. And people. Everyone . . . er . . . they left. Couldn't stomach a dead town.'

'The other houses are all empty then?' Ru glanced back. There was no community. No *we* or *us* like Gram spoke of. She was the only one left.

'Mm-hmm.' Gram grabbed the hanging weeds that had burst their way through the platform roof and were barring the way to the ticket office, sweeping them aside like a curtain. 'Just me since your gramps died. And I haven't come in here since it shut down.' She rammed the door open to a cloud of dust and insects. 'In you pop, Firecrest.' She smiled innocently at Ru, as if she were inviting her to tea. 'Go and have a little look.'

Ru stepped reluctantly inside.

Three hollow clicks were quickly followed by a sigh.

'Looks like the leccy didn't hold out,' Gram grumbled, fumbling with the light switch. 'I'll go and check the fuse box, just in case.'

Eyebrows knotted, she disappeared. Ru was left alone with the worrying sensation she'd wandered into one of Sam's apocalyptic video games. Any minute now, she'd be ravaged by zombies.

That made her more nervous than it should have.

What little she could see in the dank blackness looked kind of unimpressive. The ticket office had been turned into a tiny museum, with a gift shop plonked into the corner. Cobwebs blanketed train rubbers and magnets, and old travel posters peeled away from the wall, all branded with MID-WESSEX LINE in faded gold. Images of sailing boats bobbing on a river, an age-speckled city skyline glowing orange, and a woman posing by the shore in a swimming costume.

. . . Come to Old World Cornwall . . .
Speed to the West . . .
. . . South Wales for Bracing Holidays . . .

The smell of the ticket office was even more toxic than outside. Burnt toast and damp earth. Ru stuck her sleeve over her nose as she walked the square of the room, peering inside display cases of clouded glass.

An old stationmaster's hat. A broken lamp. Tickets and timetables and whistles. A photo of blurry people beside a blurry train. They wore coats to their shins and hats that looked like upside-down bowls, high trousers and tweed caps, waistcoats and cuffed trousers. A ringleted girl with an oversized bow clutched a doll.

MWL STAFF AND FAMILIES:
ILL-FATED TRIP TO GLASTONBURY 1925.

Ill-fated? Ru lingered on the caption, unnerved. *Why ill-fated?*

The next display case was as cloudy as if it had been dipped in milk, but its contents were still visible.

'What the—?' Ru recoiled sharply.

Inside was the skeletal remains of a cat. Its jaws were frozen mid-howl, its eye sockets hollow.

STATION NED, 1925.

Ru had a sudden urge to hug Grizabella, hairy ogre that she was. A dead cat had been sitting there for a century? This place was *way* more messed up than she'd thought.

She backed away and promptly smacked into another display case. It cracked as she collided with it, a thin line spreading from bottom to top like a lightning bolt, and something inside toppled and fell with a tinny *thunk-crack*.

Oops.

Her uncanny ability to smash into inanimate objects was as strong as ever, it seemed.

The crack snaked through the case, splitting it into two halves. In one half was a splintered violin with a single string, a rusted can labelled *Rolled Ox Tongue* – Ru gagged, and prayed it was empty – a dulled gold shoe with a damaged bow, and a familiar doll with a fractured face. Askew on the bottom was a brass pocket watch, hands frozen at 1 and 5. The glass was broken into fragments.

Was that her? Or had it already been smashed?

Not that anyone would care at this point.

The other half of the case was littered with ancient newspaper clippings and inky photographs of a mangled train. Toppled carriages lay splayed on their sides.

1 May 1925.

Ru squinted through the murk and cracks. The

headlines were clear enough, even if she couldn't make out the articles.

DAWN GLASTONBURY VIADUCT DERAILMENT. ONLY DRIVER AND STOKER SURVIVE

MELBRIDGE TRAGEDY: TRAIN CRASH KILLS ALMOST ENTIRE HAMLET

SEMAPHORE SIGNAL MISSED? QUESTIONS RAISED OVER DRIVER'S RESPONSIBILITY

Ru's stomach dropped. The ringleted girl, with her bow and little hands grasping the doll – the same broken doll in the display case – had been killed in this train crash.

Enough now. Time to go. She didn't want to see any more cat bones or death dolls.

Just as she was about to dart back to Gram's, a rustling noise came from outside.

A buzz, and the room filled with thin, yellow light.

FIVE

Ru rubbed her eyes. The darkness had cloaked the worst of her surroundings. Now she could see more weeds hanging from the ceiling and bursting through the damp walls like an alien invasion.

'The electric survived aft—' Gram strode cheerfully into the ticket office, stopping dead when she caught sight of Ru by the display case. The smile dropped from her face. 'Ah, yes. That.'

'What happened, Gram?'

A strange ghost of something hovered across Gram's expression.

'There was an accident?'

'*Ye girt gaapus*, Clara Cole.' Gram scolded herself in the old Wiltshire dialect and shuffled forward. 'I'd forgotten this was here. Yes, there was an accident.

My grandfather – Sydney – he...' she faltered. 'Do you remember I told you he only drove once? Well, he was the driver on that train. Only he and the stoker survived. Grandad got the blame, and he was never the same after that. The crash ruined him, and the shame of it trickled down to the rest of us. The curse of Melbridge, generation after generation.'

She fell silent, and the small ticket office suddenly felt like it was closing in on them. Ru needed to breathe. 'I'm gonna head back out, Gram...'

'Just let me show you something, Firecrest.'

'But I really think—'

'Come now, don't vex. It won't take more than a minute. We'll be back before your mum starts her cornflakes.'

Ignoring Ru's protests, Gram took her by the coat sleeve and half-dragged her to a corner of the ticket office. A framed map of the UK hung from the wall, covered with straight black lines and circled numbers.

'I want you to understand why it's so special here.' Gram looped Ru's arm around her own. Ru gritted her teeth and tried to quieten the alarm in her head. She wanted to escape.

'This is Melbridge, here. See?' Gram pointed to a

circle. 'With the Mid Wessex Line headquarters and steamworks. Second closest station to Avebury, one of the most magical sites on earth, and home to a sacred circle of towering stones.'

'Gram, I know what Avebury is. We passed it just before we got here and we've gone every month since I was born.'

'Right,' said Gram, triumphantly. 'And by no coincidence at all, both Avebury *and* Melbridge station lie atop one of the most powerful ley lines in the world. Do you know what's special about ley lines, Ru?'

'Not yet, Gram.' Ugh, *she* might as well have been the broken pocket watch. It felt like she'd been here for hours.

'Ley lines are ancient markers, connecting sacred sites all across the world.' Gram was already tracing her finger along the longest line on the map. 'Some believe they're conduits of magical energy, lifeblood pumping through the veins of the earth.' Her finger followed the stations from Norfolk in the east, all the way to Cornwall. The line passed straight through Avebury and Glastonbury Tor, and just skimmed Silbury Hill.

Ru straightened. She could see Silbury Hill from her old bedroom window. It stood right on the outskirts of Little Hampton. 'That's near our old house.'

'Mmm.' Gram smiled mysteriously. 'I told you; fragments of the Old Ways. They built the Mid Wessex Line to follow this ley line, so it passed through all the stations from here to Cornwall. With each train ride, each turn of the wheel, each puff of smoke, they harnessed the ancient earth power hidden deep beneath the soil.'

Ru's ears thrummed with a rush of blood. The straight, blocky line ran directly from Melbridge to Dad. Which meant the train tracks did too.

'The line runs past Little Hampton,' Ru said, the whirring cogs in her brain gathering pace. 'But all the Mid Wessex Line stations are closed now, right? All of them are gone?'

'Oh, the train tracks still remain there, underneath the mud,' Gram replied bitterly. 'But Devizes ... Holt ... Broughton Gifford Halt ... nearly all the station buildings are gone. Only a few tourist lines survive. There's even a Ritzy Rails service nearby – a team of trains that ferry posh people dressed up in

1920s garb around in the middle of the night. They make them learn the blinking Charleston. It's all *maggoty, nunny-fudgen* nonsense.'

Wiltshire slang always slipped in when Gram got wound up.

'So in theory . . .' Ru kept her voice flat. 'If you set out walking from here' – she trailed the line with her own finger – 'and followed the way of the old train tracks, you'd get all the way to the sea? And through . . .' She swallowed. 'Through all the old stops on the way?'

Gram nodded. 'That's right. Straight as a Roman road.'

Before Ru could press any further, there was a loud *POP* and what sounded like an explosion of glass breaking. The ticket office fell back into darkness.

'Curses,' Gram muttered, shuffling towards the empty lampshade. 'Well, the bulb's broken all to *flitters*. I'll clean this up, and Ru – go back home before anyone gets suspicious. Tell them I'm out worshipping the spring or something.'

'Sure, Gram.' Beyond relieved, Ru hopped over the shards of glass. In half a moment she was out in the open air, darting back along the train tracks in uncommonly steady strides.

She *finally* knew what she was going to do. And it was perfect.

six

Ru grabbed her phone from the kitchen and careered up the stairs, narrowly missing Mum as she came out of the bathroom.

'Whoooah.' Mum held Ru by the shoulders with damp hands. She smelt of her ginger shampoo. 'I thought you were still in bed. Where have you been? Where's Gram?'

'Out . . .' Ru slipped from her grasp and ducked into the box room. 'Worshipping . . . spring . . . May Eve or something . . .'

'Oh, fabulous,' Mum grimaced. 'How I've missed the New Age rubbish.'

Ru slammed the door and pulled up the map on her phone.

The disused railway line from Melbridge to Little

Hampton ran for just over three miles. Longer than by main road, but she'd never attempt that. There was no pavement, and even in her reckless frame of mind she didn't want to get flattened by a car – never mind that she'd be caught in five minutes. No way could a twelve-year-old walk alone in the dark without being cornered and forced home. She needed the back way. The shroud of secrecy.

Ru was fit – ish – and she could do three miles in an hour or so, adding in the odd ten-minute break for emergencies. A quick internet search told her that the sun would set at half past eight. Everyone would be asleep by ten, and dawn was just before six in the morning.

Nobody would have a clue she'd gone until she knocked on her old door. Dad, spending his final night in the Little Hampton house, would wake up and phone Mum, and then finally Ru could get the two of them in a room together and explain how much they should *not* split up. She'd remind them of all the good things, of everything they'd been through together, and show them pictures on her phone, like when they went to see the Red Arrows and Chippenham Folk Festival, and how they made a scarecrow for the Scarecrow Trail every autumn, but mainly she'd remind them of all those nights over the dinner table and lazy pyjama Sundays, and slowly but surely everything would fall back into place. Come morning they'd be a family again.

She smiled triumphantly to herself.

See? I can fix anything.

By the evening, her nails were nothing but jagged, pointed triangles. She'd eaten more of them than she had her dinner.

'Eat up, Rubes,' Mum urged, prodding the bowl closer to Ru. 'You like pesto pasta.'

'I'm not really hungry.'

Her phone dinged in her pocket.

It's Wednesday noodle night, Rubes.
King prawn udon here. Pad thai for u?

The picture Dad sent made her stomach growl with envy. Pink prawns and sticky red sauce in a bowl stuffed to the gills.

No noodles. Pesto pasta instead.

The three dots seemed to last forever, but Dad's reply was short.

Cool. Enjoy!

He missed the old days as much as she did. She could tell.

Not long now.

Ru packed and repacked her rucksack five times, eventually settling on a change of clothes, a flask of water, an apple, a packet of chocolate Hobnobs, Dad's old headtorch (so she didn't run down her phone battery) and her birthday money she'd been saving.

Finally, she tore a piece of paper out of her school record book and scribbled down the names of all the stations to Little Hampton. Emergency telephone numbers of Mum and Dad. Her allergies – penicillin and pineapple – just in case. She folded the paper into her pocket, poked her head round the door and checked the time on the hall clock.

Just gone half past nine.

A cloud shifted outside, and the bare window shone soft rays of twilight into the room. Dappled red light splattered the wallpaper.

'Ruby!'

There was a sudden flurry of noise outside her room, followed by several excited raps on wood.

Heart flying into her mouth, Ru kicked the bag under her bed and opened the door. 'Everything all right, Gram?'

Gram was bouncing as much as a seventy-year-old *could* bounce, wearing a yellow duffel coat on top of her dressing gown and gold sparkly wellies underneath it.

'It's a TOTAL LUNAR ECLIPSE, Firecrest! Nobody knew it was happening and it's beginning now! Come, come!'

'Er – think I just want to go to sleep, actually...'

Gram's face turned as hard as cement. 'Ruby Tanwen Darke, this has only happened once in the last century. A total lunar eclipse on May Eve is a *magical* phenomenon. I refuse to let you miss this. Outside. Now.'

She turned swiftly and marched down the stairs.

A fiery lump of panic formed in Ru's stomach, as hot as molten lava. How long did an eclipse last? Was everyone going to be up all night?

'RUBY!'

With an anxious look at the clock, Ru lumbered after Gram.

Mum was at the bottom of the stairs, wrapped in her *Hampton Morris Dancers* jumper. Her blonde bob – *spun gold*, Dad used to call it – was pushed back with a stained fabric hair band, and mascara smudges darkened the rings beneath her eyes. She'd obviously been jumped by Gram, too, because she usually managed to hide how much of a mess she'd been since the split.

Sam had been dragged out as well, even if he still had his headphones on. All he'd done the past few months was vanish. Into his phone, or his games, or his music or whatever. Each branch of her family tree was breaking off and snapping into twigs.

But it was all OK, because she was going to fix it.

Sorry, Mum mouthed.

It's fine, Ru mouthed back, despite it very much not being fine. Everyone was far from asleep. How on earth was she supposed to get out?

SEVEN

Yellow flowers were scattered on the windowsill and outside the door. Marigolds. Buttercups. Primroses, maybe. Some others Ru didn't recognize.

Gram shoved a bunch of them into her hands as they all bundled outside. 'Remember the veil thins on May Eve, Firecrest,' she warned. 'Fae and tricksters, spirits and demons . . . mark my words, they'll wander the world tonight, wreaking their chaos.'

'Ma, you'll give her nightmares,' Mum hissed.

'Oh, don't be a *muddle-fuss*, Martha.' Gram waggled her posy in the air. 'We've got protection. For all their bombast, those from the Otherworld are at the mercy of common garden plants. Flowers can summon them and they can banish them. Spirits can't cross a boundary blessed with yellow flowers.'

'Thanks, Gram.' Ru tried to sound convincingly grateful.

The others took their bunches with even less enthusiasm. Their skin was red-tinged, Ru saw, as if their blood were glowing.

'Look.' Gram's age-speckled hand lifted to the sky. 'A blood moon on May Eve.'

Ru turned her eyes upwards, and then quickly wished she hadn't.

A full moon hovered above the Melbridge tunnel, an orb of radiant pink that darkened with each second. Red, scarlet, crimson.

It felt as unnatural as the station had. Wrong.

'Folklore tells of a blood moon bringing ill fortune,' Gram murmured. 'Ancient civilizations spoke of demons invading, animals attacking, the sun and moon at war. To many, the lunar eclipse is the worst of all omens, heralding evil intent. And on May Eve, with the gateway between worlds wide open, who knows what will stalk the earth tonight?'

'Ma, stop, or I'll take the kids back inside,' Mum snapped.

Gram held her hands up in submission. 'Have it your way, Martha. It's just the Earth blocking the sun's light from the moon. Happy now?'

'Ecstatic.'

Ru peered down at her phone.

9.44 p.m.

Nervous energy whizzed round her body, and she shook her legs to release it.

'You OK there, Rubes?' She looked up to see Sam staring quizzically at her. 'You seem nervous.'

'Nope,' she gulped, stuffing her phone back in her pocket. 'Just tired.'

'You've looked at your phone like, fourteen times.'

'Oh, now you're Mr Observant? I'm waiting for Abeni to message about Games Club next week. You're not the only one with a social life, Samson.'

'If that's what you wanna call Games Club, loser,' he said, and returned his face to the sky.

It took another fifty-three minutes for everyone to go to bed, and another hour for silence to finally fall. By that time Ru's growing panic was almost unbearable. When she was sure it was safe, she zipped up her coat, picked up her rucksack and pulled the door open with a soft *creak*.

Challenge: Make it out of Gram's cottage and get

home in less than two hours. GO.

The darkness in the lounge was porridge-thick. She tapped Dad's torch with trembling fingers until the weakest beam lit up the room.

'Ah, Miss Darke. I've been expecting you.'

Ru nearly leapt out of her skin. Sam was sitting on the sofa with crossed legs, obviously trying to look like a supervillain.

'Have you been sitting with the light off this whole time, Sam? What's wrong with you?'

He ignored that. 'Rubes, it kind of looks like you're going somewhere. But you wouldn't do that, would you? Not in the middle of the night.'

The panic grew. Ru marched to the door, fumbling for the handle. 'Just . . . getting some air.'

'Huh.' Sam clicked his tongue. 'And there was me thinking you were going back to Little Hampton.' With a dramatic flick of his wrist, he produced a piece of paper and held it between two fingers. 'Forget something?'

Oh no.

Ru grasped at her pockets in alarm. Her emergency notes weren't there. They must have fallen out.

'Give that back.'

Sam made a face. 'Yeah, I don't think so. This is literally the worst idea you've ever had. What are you *thinking*? That you'll get back there, Dad'll call Mum, they'll suddenly realize they love each other again? Cancel the new tenants moving in tomorrow? It's over, Ru. They told us that, remember? They don't want to be married any more.'

'Forget the notes.' Ru opened the door, promptly hit by a shiver of cold air. 'I don't need them. I remember everything anyway.' Without looking back, she headed into the night.

'Ru, look . . . hold on . . .' A hand grabbed her arm. 'Come on, you can't do this. It's pointless and dangerous.'

Finally, the panic burst its banks and flooded her head. She didn't lose control as much as she used to, but when she did it was like a landslide; rocks splintering and plummeting at light speed.

'Smell that?' Ru yanked her arm from Sam's grasp and waved at the air, at the Melbridge stench of charred wood and burnt coal. 'That's the smell of *wrong*, Sam.' The wind caught her hair and she felt it whip behind her like flames. Any other time the drama would have been awesome. 'That smell is telling us we're in some parallel dimension where nothing's as it should be, and unless we find our way home our whole world is going to fall apart.'

'Quit the theatrics,' Sam snapped. 'Things are not that bad.'

'How can you say that? Our life and our family were perfect, and now Dad's by himself all week, we're living by a death trap, Mum's in her own world and Gram's rambling on about blood moons and ley lines. Oh, yeah, it's freaking *amazing*.'

Sam made a noise like a frustrated pig and straightened to his full height. 'Give it a rest Ruby, *please*.'

Ru stared back at him. Was Sam always that tall?

'Look, I get it,' he whispered. 'Some things suck.'

'No, Sam, *everything*...'

He raised an eyebrow, and Ru snapped her mouth shut.

'Some things suck,' he repeated in a calmer voice. 'It would be great if we had parents who loved each other and we didn't have to move out of the house. But Ru, our life before was *not* perfect.'

Ru bit down on her tongue. Unwelcome memories tried to climb, zombie-like, out of their burying place. Whispered arguments in the kitchen. Thick, horrible silences in the car. Blotchy cheeks and tear-swollen eyelids, masked with fake, shrill jokes.

No, no, no.

Ru shook the images off like dirt.

'Look, I get it. You like things how you like them, right? Noodle Night, Friday Pizza Party. Games you can win. Us four doing those annoying treasure hunts and pretending to be happy.'

Her heckles rose at that. 'We weren't pretending.'

'Maybe you weren't.' He dropped his head, ridiculous curls falling over his eyes. 'Just— stop chasing a fake memory, OK? Yeah, things are messy and yeah, I miss Dad too, but . . . I dunno. You can't control everything. Life isn't neat and perfect all the time. Maybe you've just got to strap in and ride the waves.'

And then, as if his battery had run down, his shoulders dropped. 'Or maybe that's mixed up. Dunno. But you get the point.'

So, it wasn't just Mum who had chucked their old life away like rubbish. Her brother had gone to the dark side, too.

'Please, Sam,' she whispered. 'Let me go. I'll follow the train line but won't go on the track. It's three miles, nowhere near the main road, and I'll be *so* safe. I'll leave the location tracker thingy on. I'll message you every fifteen minutes. If sixteen minutes go by and you don't hear from me, you can tell Mum. But just let me try. *Please*. If this doesn't work, I'll never go on about it again. Pinky promise.'

She held out her little finger in the way they used to. Sam looked at it, something flickering across his face.

'Ugh, whatever,' he said, and curled his own pinky round hers. 'But if you die, I get your games console.'

EIGHT

Ru gripped her rucksack straps and rounded the corner to the station. Adrenaline made her sweat, but the May night air had a bite, and she was glad of the woolly lining inside her denim jacket, of her knitted purple beret and wrist warmers.

The red moon gave the old ticket office the look of a blood-drenched skull, its eyes boarded-up windows.

I don't have to do this. I could just go back.

She glanced behind her. The thirteen houses were dark as coal.

Nope. Onwards.

Head down, torch on, she found one railway sleeper, then another. She counted them in her head as she walked alongside the track, so she wouldn't have to think about anything else or look at the endless fields that surrounded her.

She'd never known silence like it before. Fifteen minutes passed, then another, with nothing but skeletal countryside and swaying wheat.

Still alive, she messaged Sam first.

Then Am OK cow poo on fields stinks

Staring at the ground made her neck sore, so she lifted her face upwards. The surroundings had changed. Silhouettes of tall stones towered over a grass bank. Sleeping giants glittering like obsidian.

In the daylight, Avebury village was as cosy and familiar to her as her own family. By night, it felt like something else altogether. Ancient, and otherworldly. Or it would have if Ru believed in any of that stuff.

Focus, Ru. Quit spiralling.

Heart thudding, Ru turned back to the track, relieved to see something breaking through the darkness. A railway signal from the old days – a semaphore signal, Mum had told her once – stood above, with an arm pointing diagonally down, and a feeble green light shining.

That meant *ALL CLEAR. GO.*

A little way ahead sat a small, slatted hut, crumbling and forgotten, with two unlit windows dense with cobwebs.

Avebury Halt Signal Box.

Nerves abandoned, Ru pumped the air with her fist. If the signal box was here, the station couldn't be far away.

Melbridge, Avebury Halt, Little Hampton.

Halfway home. She was actually *doing it*. Her careful tread turned into a run, and she skipped beside the train tracks, feeling lighter than she had in months. The night mist even seemed to dance through the air like a plume of steam.

And then came the first sound.

A squeak, a creak – like the opening of an old door behind her.

Ru stopped dead. Adrenaline raced to her limbs.

It could be an owl. A fox. Foxes could scream like they were being murdered. But no, that wasn't an animal. That sounded like machinery.

The prolonged *creak* stopped, followed quickly by the second noise – a *THUNK* – as if something had clicked into place. Then silence.

Trying to swallow the dry mass of fear forming in

her throat, Ru held her thumb over the buttons on her phone, ready to dial for help, and slowly spun round.

Nothing there.

She exhaled shakily. There was only the empty signal box. But the tall semaphore signal had changed. It now pointed straight out to the side, and was glowing as red as the moon.

CAUTION. SLOW.

Ru glared at it in confusion. She was absolutely *positive* the signal had been facing down a moment ago, with a green light. And there was nobody inside the signal box to operate it.

So how . . . ?

The third sound was from right in front of her. Louder than thunder it came, cutting through the night like a banshee's scream.

A-wooooo.

The shock made Ru lose her footing, and she stumbled into the bank of grass alongside the tracks.

What *was* that?

The night was suddenly soupy, smoke merging with the mist. She couldn't see beyond the end of her nose.

A-wooooo. A ghostly, discordant wail.

Crouching low, Ru followed the twisting curve of the train tracks, craning her neck, heron-like. Around the curve was a neat wooden platform, with a bench and a hanging basket of flowers. And, there, waiting patiently at the platform edge, was an old-fashioned steam train, gleaming like an emerald, with three carriages trailing elegantly behind. Smoke curled above it in a question mark.

Stifling a yell, Ru wobbled out of her crouching position and fell flat on to her backside.

A pair of legs in spotless black trousers – cuffs turned up neatly at the ankle – descended the steps of the train, alighted on to the platform and walked carefully towards the bank where Ru lay. Too scared to lift her head, she followed the tread of two perfectly laced-up shoes. When she finally looked up, she saw a man bending over her, his eyes an unblinking bolt of blue.

'Are you all right, miss?'

Was he concerned? Angry? Something else?

Ru gaped at him, stuck like glue to the grass. She couldn't read his expression.

'I . . . I fell over.'

He chuckled, his cheeks dimpling.

Phew. Not anger, then.

'Yes, I noticed that.' His Wiltshire lilt was stronger than her own, but his voice was as soft as a dandelion clock.

Ru twisted herself to sitting and took the stranger in. He was lit by the train lamp and dressed in vintage uniform – a long tailcoat and a smartly pressed waistcoat, the chain of a pocket watch passed through his buttonhole. His moustache was neatly curled up at the ends, sitting underneath a long, pointed nose and sea-pool eyes that crinkled at the edges. He looked somehow both teenage and middle-aged at the same time, but then she'd always sucked at guessing how old people were. A brass ring of keys jangled at his side, and there was a golden insignia on the rim of his hat and shoulders. *MWL*. Mid Wessex Line.

'Give me a minute,' Ru said from the ground, trying to steady her breath. 'Bit shocked.' Her eyes slid to the train, magnificent and moonlit. It seemed to be watching her. It had to be one of the *'maggoty, nunny-fudgen nonsense'* things Gram had mentioned. 'Is that a Ritzy Rails train?'

'Interesting.' The man paused, regarding her.

'Care to tell me what you know of the Ritzy Rails service, miss?'

'My Gram told me it was where people get dressed up in old-fashioned clothes and ride on a train by moonlight. And they make you learn the Charleston.'

He laughed. 'That's right. I'm the Conductor. Mr Cribbins.'

'Ruby. Ru. Ru Darke.'

'Darke? Your name is Darke?' He looked momentarily taken aback. 'Forgive me, but that is a fairly unusual name to find in Wiltshire.'

'My dad's not from here,' Ru replied. 'Mum is, though.'

'Ah.' The Conductor's face relaxed. 'And may I ask what you're doing here? It's a strange place to find a young wanderer in the middle of the night.'

'Well . . .' An ember of an idea sparked in Ru's brain and she got to her feet.

Challenge: Get a ride home. GO.

'I'm heading back to Little Hampton village – my dad's meeting me there . . .' She added the last bit, just to be safe. 'But I'm kind of regretting walking, to be honest.'

'Well...' Cribbins pulled his watch chain from his pocket, and it made a faintly insistent *tick-tock*. He stared into the clock face before glancing back at the waiting train. 'We're due at Little Hampton in fourteen minutes. It's the next stop. Care to jump aboard?'

'Oh, wow!' Ru tried to look surprised. 'Do you know, that didn't even cross my mind? It's so kind of you, but I haven't got a ticket or anything...' She rummaged in her pockets. 'I've got £20, but if that's not enough I can send some more once I'm back home...'

Cribbins' eyes twinkled like sapphires. With a twitch of his moustache, he reached into his waistcoat and pulled out a brown square ticket printed with old-fashioned ink. 'Just don't tell the other passengers you got a free ride, understand?'

```
1 May
Avebury Halt
First Class Single TO any MWL station
```

'First class?' Ru whistled. 'The closest I've ever come to first class is getting lost at Düsseldorf airport.'

That made Cribbins smile. 'Happy to oblige.'

If he weren't a total stranger, Ru would've hugged him. She'd be home in a matter of minutes, with no tripping over nettles and thistles, or jumping at every random sound. With any luck, Dad would still be awake watching *Doctor Who*.

'Thank you,' she said gratefully, and as if it had heard her, the train whistled in reply.

'I think that's our cue.' Cribbins turned towards the platform. 'She gets into a sulk if we're not on time. Come along, miss. *The Green Lady* is waiting.'

NINE

Ru followed him cautiously, eyeing *The Green Lady* as if it were a skittish horse about to bolt. She'd never seen an actual steam train in real life before, and it was *gigantic*. So much bigger than the modern electric ones, with its wheels as large as her, and MID WESSEX LINE emblazoned in gold. Steampunk central, a mass of brass cogs and levers.

The train's face was a black circle, with a pristine number plate. 0505. Two levers pointed like the hands of a clock, and the train whispered *chuff-chuff* in her ear.

'Miss?' Cribbins opened a door and a green velvet carpet unrolled down the steps. 'Welcome aboard.'

Tick-tock.

Ru's trainers sank into the carpet as she climbed

up, landing in a mahogany corridor softly lit by oil lamps. Dozens of excited voices floated through from the other two coaches: young, old and everything in between. Somebody somewhere was playing a jig on the violin.

'It seems pretty full,' Ru said doubtfully. She didn't want to chat to champagne-giggly adults. They always wanted to ask her stuff, like how school was going and what hobbies she had, and tell her how chunky mobile phones used to be.

Cribbins leapt up behind her, rolling up the carpet as he went. 'I'm sure there's a corner we can squeeze you into.' He swung the door shut. 'If you'd care to follow me.'

She trailed him obediently through the corridor until he paused outside another door. COACH C.

Tick-tock.

Snatches of the violin music floated towards them, and there came a quiver of bells. Someone laughed amid the chatter. This Ritzy Rails service was clearly *packed*, and Ru braced herself for the onslaught of stares.

'Do head in, miss,' Cribbins said, wrapping one hand around the door handle. 'Allow *The Green*

Lady to ferry you the rest of the way in comfort. Please help yourself to anything on offer, but I must ask you to abide by two rules. The first: please do not touch the vases, or their contents. The second: do not try and leave your carriage. Safety reasons, you understand. I will ensure you have everything you could possibly need inside.'

'Got it.' Ru was itching for the journey to begin. 'No flowers, stay put. Can I go in now?'

'Of course.' Cribbins held the door open. 'Settle in, and I'll be back to stamp your ticket once we're off.' He touched the rim of his hat with his finger.

The moment Ru lifted her foot over the doorway, the music and voices cut off mid-strain, leaving nothing but yawning silence.

The coach glimmered with lamplight. Rows of tables were lined up next to the windows, draped in ice-white tablecloths. Vases of bluebells and cream blossoms stood primly on each one – *absolutely mustn't touch those, remember, Ru* – and plush green and gold armchairs tucked in either side. A boy and a girl, both about her age, were seated at opposite ends of the carriage, very much avoiding each other's eye. The other chairs were empty.

Where had everybody else gone?

The carriage door slammed shut, and she jumped.

'Er, hi.' She gulped and attempted to flatten her hair, which sprang out further than ever. 'What happened to the other people? I heard a load of noise.'

There was a long minute of nothing, until finally the girl's head poked out from the far table. 'Ah yeah, it's from one of the other carriages, I guess. We can only hear it when the train slows.' She stared at Ru, chewing her lip like it was made of toffee. 'Is it OK if I say hi to you?'

'Course it is! Why wouldn't it be?'

The girl made her way to Ru in long, confident strides, adorned with rainbow-coloured hair and stripey dungarees. A DSLR camera was looped round her neck, and a sweet scent of cherry came with her.

'Y'know, some people are shy. Which is TOTALLY VALID,' she said, throwing a look to the boy. 'So it's always good to ask. I'm Elfie. It's short for Elfleda. Elfleda Midwinter.'

'Elfleda Midwinter?'

'Yeah, gotta love a weird surname *and* a weird first name, right?' she grinned. 'My mums like history,

Elfleda was this epic medieval queen – it's a whole thing. Sorry, what's your name?'

'I'm . . .' Before Ru could introduce herself, Elfie had thrown her arms around her ribs in a concertina-like squeeze. 'I'm Ruby,' she squeaked. 'Ru.'

Immediately, Elfie withdrew. 'Sorry, Ruby Ru,' she smiled apologetically. Her teeth were dotted with blue train-track braces. 'I always forget to ask for a hug. Mam has to remind me. She's a spiritual psychologist, but the rest of my family are folk musicians and we hug *everyone*.'

'Don't worry about it.' Ru's breath flooded back, and she placed her bag on the closest seat. 'Tight hugs are good. Soft hugs, though – they're the devil's work.'

Elfie broke into a charming, sun-wide smile. 'Gotcha. Bear hugs for Ru, then. My brother's the same.'

At the mention of a brother, Ru's stomach twisted. *Oh, no.* How much time had passed since she'd last messaged Sam? Was Mum chasing after her as they spoke? Was she at the platform now, convincing the Conductor to let her on, too?

'I should message my brother and let him know

where I am.'

She took out her phone. No signal. Not even one tiny bar. And the battery was at two per cent, despite her charging it up before she left. Stupid thing. Well, Sam'd just have to wait until she got to Little Hampton. Even if he had told Mum, Ru would be with Dad by the time she caught up. No need to spiral.

Weird, though.

'I had full battery and signal outside. None in here and my phone's about to die.'

'Mine too,' Elfie said. 'What about you?' She turned back to the silent boy. He looked smart, Ru noted; bookish, as if he spent most of his time in the library. Was he vaguely familiar, or was she imagining it?

He wore a white shirt, an unbuttoned waistcoat and linen trousers. It was sort of old-fashioned; most likely a private school uniform. No chance she'd met him before. She didn't know anyone who dressed like that.

His hands were clamped tightly together. 'What about me what?' he said, forehead furrowed.

'Your phone. Is it working?'

'I . . .' It sounded like it pained him to talk. 'I don't have one.'

'Ah, right.' Ru sank into the closest armchair and stared out the window. A new haze of stars littered the red sky. She'd only be out of service for a while. It was fine. Still felt strange though, nobody knowing where she was; like she'd jumped out of the real world for a bit. And her pulse was *still* racing. Her pesky nervous system clearly hadn't twigged that she was safe.

All at once came another scream of the whistle, and the train jerked to life. Ru gripped the edges of her chair as steam billowed past her window, insistent *chuff-chuffs* gathering speed as *The Green Lady* left Avebury Halt station and carried them into the night.

Ten

Gathering steam swiftly painted the windows, swallowing up the night sky, the blood moon and all the stars. They could be anywhere and nowhere.

It was like their Düsseldorf flight. Eight-year-old Ru had been so excited to fly for the first time, but as soon as their plane had risen into the clouds, she'd wanted to go back home. The endless sea of white and the total lack of safe ground had brought on one of her landslides, and Mum and Dad had curled their hands around her own. *'Keep holding on to us,'* Dad had said. *'Me and Mum. We'll be your guiding lights.'*

She wasn't scared this time, though. She was her own guiding light.

Just as he'd promised, Cribbins appeared soon

after they left, accompanied by the *tick-tock* of his watch. In his hand he grasped a two-handled metal thing, not unlike a pair of pliers. 'Tickets please.'

Ru and Elfie held theirs out in unison, but he took the ticket punch to the boy first. 'Malik Marley. Have you found your ticket yet?'

The boy – Malik – fumbled in his waistcoat pocket. 'No. I . . . I will find it. I promise. I think perhaps my mother has it? She's . . . she's in the other coach. Perhaps . . . perhaps I can go and get it from her?'

Cribbins glared at him coldly, and the lamplight flickered.

'I see.' His reply was a shard of ice. 'Do not move from the seat until you find it. I will be keeping an eye on you. Do you understand?'

'Y-yes,' Malik said weakly. 'Yes.'

'Yes what?'

'Yes, sir.'

Unnerved, Ru watched Cribbins turn away. His reaction seemed a touch out of line, and kind of unexpected. After all, *she* hadn't had a ticket before the Conductor gave her one. What was the issue with Malik?

There was a muted *click* and Ru's eye flicked to a small movement. Unseen to the others, Elfie had taken a photograph.

'Miss Midwinter!' A spin of the ticket punch, and Cribbins looked normal again. 'May I see your ticket?'

See? Everything's fine, Ru told herself sternly. *Stop looking for trouble.*

Elfie handed it over, and Cribbins took it, pinching it with his fingernails so he was barely touching it. He considered it with owl-like concentration, nodded, and punched through it with a *snap*. It left a cutout of a tiny crescent moon. Then finally, it was Ru's turn.

'Hardly worth it for such a short journey, right?' Ru grinned, as the punch stamped through hers, leaving the same moon-shaped hole. 'I'll be getting off in a minute.'

Cribbins lifted his eyes from the ticket and smiled, showing the dimple on his cheek. 'If you say so, miss.'

Huh, Ru thought, as she tucked the ticket back in her pocket. *That was a strange thing to say.*

No. That wasn't fair. Why did she keep searching

for holes that weren't there? She'd got a free ride, and her brain needed to shut up and be grateful. Besides, she'd be off in a matter of minutes.

And now he was speaking. *Focus, Ru.*

'... hungry ...' Cribbins was saying. 'Allow me to provide you with a small token of our appreciation for choosing *The Green Lady*, compliments of the Mid Wessex Line.' He disappeared around the doorway for a moment, then reappeared pushing an elegantly ornate trolley, overflowing with the most magnificent food she'd ever seen. The carriage filled with a thousand delicious scents, and Ru realized how painfully hungry she was. Never mind the chocolate Hobnobs – this'd do nicely.

She didn't have to force herself to focus any more. She was practically drooling over the mountain of goodies.

'Oh my *days*.' Elfie scrambled off her seat, snapping multiple pictures as she ogled. 'Is this all for us? Can ... can we have more than one thing?'

'Nobody else will be joining you.' Cribbins' cheeks bloomed with pride. 'Help yourself to all of it; indeed, everything this carriage contains is at your disposal. And when you've got everything you need, there's no need to leave at all, is there?' With a tip of his hat he ducked out, closing the door gently behind him.

Operation Reunite Family was rapidly turning out to be Ru's best idea *ever*. She filled a plate with clotted cream scones, cinnamon buns and strawberry Danishes, neatly cut triangles of cucumber-and-cream-cheese sandwiches, blueberry muffins and velvety chocolate mousses.

'You're not eating, Malik?' she asked, a pastry already halfway to her mouth.

'No.'

Suit yourself. Ru shrugged. Why anyone would ever pass up the opportunity to stuff their faces was beyond her, but Malik was probably still feeling bad over the whole ticket thing.

'There are hot drinks in the pots!' Elfie cried, peering over her own towering collection. 'And cold drinks underneath!'

Ru ran her eyes over each pot – green ceramic with painted gold roses, and labelled in cursive writing.

Hot Chocolate
Mint and Nettle
Ginger and Lemon

The cold drinks were in glass bottles, corked at the top.

Dandelion and Burdock
Rose Lemonade
Elderberry Cordial

'I think I've died and gone to heaven,' said Elfie. 'I actually really do.'

Ru paused, her mouth full of blueberry muffin. Elfie's words sent an inexplicable shudder right through her.

She wasn't Gram; it wasn't like she was going to start throwing salt over her left shoulder or knocking on wood, but Elfie's throwaway mention of death twanged a nerve, and she had no idea why. It was as if a stone had landed in her belly.

'You shouldn't say that,' she mumbled. 'Don't say that.'

Elfie, nose-deep in chocolate mousse, hadn't even heard. Malik had, though; Ru felt his inscrutable glare follow her as she sat back down and poured rose lemonade into a crystal glass.

Winter time has gone and past-o

'Hey, listen!' Ru held up a finger. 'D'ya hear that?'

The music began once more, with the ringing of bells and the violin's folksy melody. This time though, somebody was singing along.

Summer time has come at last-o
We shall sing and dance the day...

'Is that the Charleston?' Ru frowned.

Somebody laughed merrily. Muffled voices bellowed, hands clapped and feet stamped in rhythm.

'Course not,' Malik replied, without looking over. 'The Charleston is jazz music. This is a local folk tune.'

And come followin' the Green Man that brings
the May...

'Told you, it comes and goes.' Crumbs sprayed from Elfie's mouth. 'We can only hear it whenever we're near a station.'

'It sounds like they're having a party.' Ru put her ear against the door. It didn't sound any closer. 'Very much *not* my kind of party. You didn't want to join in either?'

'No,' said Malik.

'Nah, you're all right,' Elfie chuckled drily, sending another fountain of crumbs to the carpet. 'Spontaneous folk jams are a daily thing at home. I'm enjoying the quiet.'

As if on cue, *The Green Lady*'s whistle screamed, cutting through the music like a knife. The party noise stopped abruptly.

'Thanks, whistle.' Elfie raised her cup of hot chocolate. 'Peace.'

The gaps between *chuff-chuffs* grew longer as the train started to brake. Ru peered out the window. She could just make out the shape of a platform, and a sign wrapped with billows of pink-tinged smoke. Her stomach churned with excitement. She'd known it was the next stop. She'd written it in her notes. Cribbins had said. But it still came as a shock. She'd actually *done* it.

Little Hampton.

In a heartbeat she'd be at home with Dad, and everything would be OK.

Before she could think too much about what was coming, Ru gathered up her bag and jacket. 'That's my stop,' she said. 'It's been a total pleasure riding with you.'

Elfie saluted. 'Till we meet again, compadre.'

'Ruby . . .' Malik piped up, the loudest he'd been. 'I don't . . . I mean, I'd . . . are you positive the train's stopping?' His voice split with a dry crack.

'Positive.' Ru waved at the window. 'You can see the platfor—'

But even through the mist, she could see the platform was gliding away from her, out of frame. It vanished into the smoke.

'What?' Ru glued her nose to the window, trying to catch sight of something. Anything. The *chuff-chuffs* gathered speed again, racing and tripping over each other, faster and faster.

'No, no, no, that's not right.'

She staggered back and forth with the train, grasping at the air.

The Green Lady had missed her stop.

ELEVEN

Ru was trying *really hard* not to panic, but the oil lamps were suddenly too bright. The repetitive *chuff-chuffs* burrowed into her brain and blood, leaving her insides all raw and gritty. She cracked her knuckles, again and again, but that didn't calm her down like it usually did.

Still no signal on her phone. Nothing at all. Even the phone clock wasn't working – stuck on 10.31 p.m. when she'd last messaged Sam.

As a last, spiteful act, the battery reached zero per cent and promptly died with a sad *beep-bloop*.

Her family were going to kill her. Like, properly kill her dead, and that was hardly going to fix things, was it? Her beautiful plan was crumpling in front of her eyes, tearing into tiny papery shreds.

'Don't you dare freak out,' she muttered to herself. 'It's fine. Don't freak out.'

'Is she talking to us?' Malik frowned.

'I don't think so,' said Elfie. 'Give her a moment.'

Ru screwed up her eyes and tried to picture the next stops she'd written down on the emergency notes Sam had found, but the only thing she could think about was it terminating in Cornwall, and if she ended up there, she'd be literally HUNDREDS of miles from home, and she'd be in so much trouble she'd probably be barred from Games Club for all time and her parents would be further apart than ever.

She took a deep breath. *Dragon breaths*, Mum called them, for when her feelings got too big for her body. 'Well, I'll just have to get off at the next stop, I guess. Anyone know what it is? When are you two getting off?'

Elfie speedily gulped down a mouthful of chocolate. 'I . . . I don't know . . .'

Malik's lips had paled. He didn't say anything.

'Right. Right.' Ru stomped over the growing unease. 'Which carriage are your families in? Can we ask them?'

'Oh, but . . .' Elfie suddenly looked anxious. 'My

family isn't on the train. We're on holiday from Northumberland – we're from round here, see, generations back, and my mam wanted a nose around. They left me behind for the evening when they went out, so I thought *suit yourselves* and went on my own adventure. Saw the train, the Conductor gave me a free ticket, and it's fine because he told me the tracks are just on a loop, y'know, like at theme parks. The train's heading back round soon, I just don't know exactly when.'

That didn't sound right. Ru's ears rang with Gram's description of the line: *Straight as a Roman road.*

'Elfie, when did you get on?'

'A couple of stations before you did – Ogbourne St George – but you really don't need to panic, Ru. Mr Cribbins told me – it's on a loop.'

'Elfie, it's not on a loop,' Ru croaked. 'There's no way it can be, I've seen the map. The track goes for hundreds of miles. East to west, right across the country.'

Elfie sat heavily in an armchair. Her china cup slipped through clammy fingers, and cocoa sprayed the white cloth. 'Oh my days.'

'And you're totally on your own?'

A fervent nod of the head. Her teeth were chattering, Ru saw, her train-track braces glittering.

'And Malik?' Ru turned to him. 'When were you supposed to get off? You said your mum was on board. Where's she?'

'I . . . lied,' Malik muttered, and Ru's eyes dropped to his hands – hands gripping the seat so hard that his fingers had blanched underneath the nails.

Chills zigzagged down her back. Malik's intensity made Ru nervous. But intense people always did. *Too sensitive*, her teachers called her.

'It's only me. That is . . . I'm not . . . not quite sure why . . .' Malik's sentences evaporated into steam, as if they were too light for him to hold. 'It's all muddled now, because I was so frightened, but I told Mr Cribbins I'd lost my ticket, and he let me ride while I looked for it, but I didn't have one and I didn't know what he'd do if he realized . . . but then the train didn't stop, only to let you two on, but anyway he says there's only one stop that I'm allowed to get off at, and I can't leave and I don't know why . . . and I should have told you, I'm so, so sorry, I wanted to, but . . .' He scrunched his fingers through his hair, and tears pooled in the corner of his eyes.

'Malik . . .' Ru said quietly. 'How long have you been on here?'

'I don't know. A long time. Hours, maybe.'

'What?' Ru and Elfie swapped alarmed looks. 'Hours?'

'That's why you were so quiet,' Elfie said softly. 'You must've been in a total state.'

Ru stared incredulously. Malik knew? He knew there was something wrong and he still let them get on?

Malik looked down at his boots. 'I'm so sorry. I should have told you.'

You really should have, Ru's brain snapped.

'Don't worry,' she said tightly.

'Malik, you were scared.' Elfie budged into the seat next to him, and he pulled his hand away from her outreached one. 'Don't you *dare* punish yourself. None of us think straight when we're frightened. We'll figure it out. Won't we, Ru?'

She gave Ru a steely gaze.

'Of course we will.' Unsure of what else to do, Ru sat back down at the table and took a glug of the rose lemonade. It tasted like petrol now. Her appetite had completely vanished.

'See? Nobody's angry with you.' Elfie's smile was warm, and Malik repaid it with a crooked one of his own.

Ru breathed dragon-deep again, determinedly pushing her bad thoughts away. She couldn't afford to lose control. Not now. 'So, none of us have anyone else on board?' she asked.

Two small nods.

'And nobody knows where we are?'

Two even smaller nods.

'And we've got no idea where this train is going or when it's going to stop?'

The slightest of twitches.

'Oh, good.' Head spinning, Ru closed her eyes and let that sink in. 'I see. Well at least we know what's what. That's always an advantage.'

TWELVE

Ru turned the situation over in her mind, upside down and inside out, and tried to summon Dad's calm logic. What did he always say when her anxiety got the better of her?

'Work with what's happening, Rubes. Not what might happen. Look at what is, not what if. That's much easier to fix.'

What is. Not what *if*.

'Well,' she announced decidedly. 'There's only one thing we can do. We have to speak to the Conductor and find out where we're stopping next.'

Two doubtful faces stared back at her.

'I mean . . .' Elfie's mouth twisted in thought. 'I guess that's the only option. Do you think we can trust him, though?'

Ru waved that off. 'I'm sure it'll be OK. It'll just be a misunderstanding, and we're panicking, that's all. Cribbins works for the train company – he's hardly a lone wolf going rogue, is he? They'll be monitoring every Ritzy Rails ride, you'll see.'

'The Ritzy what?' Malik looked perplexed.

'Malik, you know.' Ru cracked her knuckles impatiently. 'The old train service with the Charleston and the party and stuff. Honestly, it'll all be a stupid mistake, and we'll be laughing about it in less than an hour.'

Elfie's shoulders relaxed. 'You're right, Ru. Of course you're right. It's all just a misunderstanding, isn't it? We'll be home soon, won't we?'

'Elfie, I'll bet you a tenner we'll be back in our beds before midnight.'

Malik didn't say anything.

Darkness flashed as they sped through a tunnel, and suddenly Cribbins was standing in the doorway.

Tick-tock.

Ru let out a shriek, unable to mask her shock. 'When did—' she spluttered, 'how . . . ?'

How had he got in? The door was closed. It hadn't opened. Had it?

'I didn't hear him come in,' Elfie whispered. 'Did you?'

Ru shook her head.

In the dim light, the Conductor's eye sockets seemed to sink into themselves. As if they were empty. As if his head were only a skull.

Tick-tock.

Ru was frozen to the spot.

They left the tunnel as quickly as they'd entered it, and Cribbins' bony face turned human again. It did funny things, darkness.

Calm down, Ru. It's nothing.

'I rather have a habit of arriving unannounced.' Cribbins smiled under his perfect moustache. 'Did I frighten you?'

Ru swallowed. It wasn't like her to be this jumpy.

'I trust you enjoyed your refreshments?'

Ask him, Ru. What are you waiting for? Do it now.

'Delicious, thanks.' Ru forced herself to sound breezy.

'An honour, truly.' Cribbins grasped the trolley handle and began to back away.

'Wait!' Ru found herself on her feet. Oddly, her legs were shaking. 'Can I . . . can I ask you a question?'

In her peripheral vision she saw Elfie and Malik, watching like hawks.

Cribbins fixed her with a sincere look. 'Of course you can, miss. I'm here to assist. How may I help?'

'It's just...' Her throat was oddly thick. Why was she so terrified? *Stop being an idiot.* 'We went past my stop. And Elfie wants to head back home, and Malik was only planning on being here for a short time and he's been here for hours...'

'Hours?' Cribbins shot Malik a veiled look. It lasted only a second, but Ru was certain she caught a glimpse of undiluted hatred. By the time she'd clocked it, though, his expression had changed. 'Mr Marley informed you he's been on board for hours, did he?'

'I... I'm sure it's just been a mistake,' Ru went on, 'but can we get off at the next station? And maybe... maybe you can phone our families to let them know where we are?'

A beat. Then the Conductor lifted his hat and ran a hand smoothly through his hair, oily and brown, shining slickly beneath the oil lamps. 'I don't understand, miss,' he said, frowning.

Ru's heart fell. 'But...'

'*The Green Lady* has only one stop left.' Suddenly Cribbins' blue eyes were as dead and cold as frosted glass. 'And you promised not to leave Coach C, remember? Besides, it's not as if you'd want to leave. You have everything you need here.'

'Only one stop?' It was hard to breathe. 'Which stop?'

Cribbins ignored her and pulled the key chain from his waist. 'I'll leave you all to your revelry – duty calls, you understand – but I do so hope you enjoy your ride on *The Green Lady*.'

And with that, he placed his hat back on his head and wheeled the trolley outside, locking the door with an ominous *clank*.

The whistle came a few moments later, like the howl of a wolf at the moon.

THIRTEEN

'No way.' Ru strode to the door. 'He's not allowed to keep us locked in like this. It's against the law. If I can just open . . . *OW!*' She whipped her fingers away from the handle as a searing pain scalded her skin.

'You OK?' Elfie was up and by her side. 'Ru, your hand! What happened?'

A fresh burn had imprinted itself across her palm. 'The door handle was *boiling*. Like sticking my hand in fire.'

Without waiting for instruction, Elfie solemnly took a water bottle from her bag, poured some on to a napkin and held it against Ru's skin. 'Don't move.'

Ru sucked air through her teeth. The mark had sliced her skin in two, and it didn't look like any burn she'd ever had. And yet it was healing already.

Elfie paused her daubing. When she spoke, her voice was low. 'Ru, I'm starting to think there's something unnatural going on.'

'Eh? What do you mean?'

'Well . . .' She hesitated and flicked her eyes to Malik. 'I don't want to scare anyone, but not strictly *of this realm*, if you get my drift.'

'Oh.' Ru scoffed. She didn't mean to. 'Right.'

Malik twitched and pressed himself against the window like a frightened puppy. 'What? You think what?' He crossed his trembling fingers. 'They've . . . they've warned us about things like this at church. It's May Day, Elfie; strange things happen on May Day and we've some strange customs in the west, Elfie, like the White Horses and the Green Man, what if . . . ?'

'Malik, calm down!' Ru removed her hand from Elfie's grasp. 'There's nothing *unnatural* going on here. Cribbins is just some loser on a power trip.'

'Do you really think so, Ru?' Elfie said softly, sounding just like Gram when she was going on about crystal runes or star signs.

'Course he is. That stuff's not real, Elfie.'

'What else would cause that mark on your hand? That is *not* a normal burn. Look, it's practically gone already.'

Ru could feel the bubble of a cynical retort, so she took herself to the window and leant her forehead against the glass. The silent countryside sped past in a blur. They were chugging next to fields fenced by a row of overhanging trees. The wind teased swathes of leaves from the branches, and they spun and danced in the bloody moonlight.

At last, a dark mound shrouded in scarlet shadow passed by the window.

Silbury Hill.

The view from her old bedroom.

Home.

The longing was so visceral she could almost see it – a knotted rope yanking at her organs.

And then she actually *was* yanked, as an unexpected force pulled her from the window.

'What—?' Ru began, but a shockwave smashed her chest and sent her flying. With an *ooft* she fell backwards, tumbling to the floor with Elfie beside her. In the pale red light, she saw the same fear-stricken expression.

The lights spluttered off, and then on again, until finally they blew, throwing the train into blackness.

'Is everyone OK?' she called.

'Has there been an accident?' Malik croaked in the dark. 'Are we dead?'

Tick-tock.

Cribbins was nowhere to be seen, but Ru was certain she could hear his pocket watch. It slipped between the train's *chuffs* in jarring discord.

Tick-tock.

The lamps exploded back to life, glaring like spotlights.

'We're not dead,' she panted, and pulled herself to her feet. The lights settled and the train was steady again, blithely chugging along like nothing had happened. 'Just a broken bit of track or something.'

Outside the window, the rosy, moonlit shapes of Silbury Hill, and a little further behind, the stones of Avebury, perched on the edge of the horizon.

Elfie appeared at her shoulder, hair and dungarees in disarray. 'Looks sort of like a gateway to another dimension, doesn't it?' she whispered. 'Perhaps that's what caused the bump.'

Ru rolled her eyes and dropped on to an armchair, rubbing the new bruises that were forming. Elfie was way, way off track, obviously. Clearly there was nothing supernatural going on, but it *did* feel like they'd entered a new world. An unknown, unsafe one in which Ru had no control of what happened next, and she could only watch the old world move further and further out of reach.

The carriage suddenly seemed impossibly small and airless. Squeezing the life out of them.

Dragon breaths, Ru.

She imagined Mum sitting patiently beside her until the bad things passed. Ginger shampoo and chai lattes. Dad on the other side, wonderfully practical, his RELAX, I HAVE A SPREADSHEET FOR THAT mug clasped in his hands.

Deal with what IS, Rubes. Not what IF.

Feelings versus logic. The constant Cole/Darke battle.

She knew which one she had to listen to right now.

'I swear there's *nothing* paranormal going on.' Jaw determinedly set, Ru rose and reached gingerly for the handle again. Warm but not hot, like a kettle that had cooled. And disappointingly, it was still locked. 'See? It's all right now. Y'know, there's a lot of things that could cause a hot door handle. Dodgy power supply, for example, or magnetic locks. I'm sure someone'll sort it out. Cribbins, or . . .'

Wait.

'Hang on . . .' She spun back to see Elfie and Malik gazing expectantly at her. 'Nobody can run a train on their own, can they? Have we seen any other crew members yet? Heard from the driver?'

'Um . . .' Elfie considered it for a moment. 'No. Only the Conductor.'

'Malik?'

'Not a soul.' Malik's fingers were still crossed. 'I haven't seen anyone. I've only heard the other passengers through the walls.'

Of course! Ru could've kicked herself. 'The other carriages! I'm such an idiot. Even if we can't find any other crew, there are loads of other people on board. They're too busy having a party to notice what's going on right now, but we can tell them and they'll help us sort this out.'

'But how can you tell them when you can't open the door?' began Malik, swiftly interrupted by Ru dumping her bag upside down, its contents spilling on to the table.

'We're going to slip them a note. Anyone got a pen?'

FOURTEEN

'I've got my camera, fruity chewing gum and my sister's cherry lip balm.' Elfie chucked the contents of her pockets next to Ru's things. 'Malik?'

'Um . . . I was sure I had something . . .' he said distractedly, 'but I can't remember . . .'

Ru opened her mouth to press him but quickly decided against it. Malik hardly seemed the type of boy to carry practical stuff anyway.

'And I've got biscuits, a headtorch and twenty quid,' she sighed instead. 'Nothing to write with.' She took a quick sweep of the coach. 'But I'd bet there's a pad or pen somewhere. There were pens and posh paper in our hotel in Düsseldorf. My brother kept writing swear words on them. All fancy places have them, don't they?'

Elfie chuckled wryly. 'When we go somewhere other than an electricity-free farm for our holidays, I'll let you know.'

'I've only been on holiday once,' Malik added unexpectedly. 'We went to Weston-super-Mare when Dad was on leave from the army. It wasn't fancy, and there was no stationery. But it was nice. We went in the sea.' He smiled at the memory. It was a nice smile, Ru thought, and she wished he'd wear it more often. It made him look more human and less anxious robot.

'What about the luggage cabinets?' Elfie suggested. 'He said everything in Coach C was at our disposal, didn't he?'

'There's luggage in here? Where?'

'Up there.' Elfie pointed at the trio of cabinets that ran above the windows, and clambered on to a chair. Her dungarees lifted at the ankles and revealed beautiful hand-painted Doc Martens. Elfie was a real artist. Intricate swirls and runes, colourful Celtic symbols and words in a language Ru didn't understand.

Elfie would be Gram's dream grandkid. That thought burnt like a hot poker, because Ru would literally do *anything* to hear some of Gram's bizarre hippy stuff right now.

What would her family be doing? Had Sam told them what was going on? Had they called the police? Had anyone even noticed?

Shake it off. Head in the game.

'Oh my days!' Elfie opened the first cabinet. 'There are loads of suitcases here.' She glanced down at Ru, offering her a cheeky grin. 'Maybe they're full of gorgeous vintage stuff. What do you think about a little dress-up?'

Ru made a face and climbed on to the opposite chair. 'You do you, Elfie,' she grunted, stretching to reach the next cabinet handle. Elfie was at least a year older than her, and a little bit taller. 'Any time I wear a dress I fall over. I wouldn't be caught dead in one of these.'

A strange shiver made its way up her back. *Caught dead.*

She felt the burn of Malik's eyes on her and flinched as she saw a similar sensation painted all over his face. Haunted.

'Don't you want to look too, Malik?' she asked, not unkindly. 'I'm sure you don't actually have to stay in that seat for the whole journey.'

'Perhaps you're right,' he said, but he didn't move.

Ru and Elfie began lifting the bags on to the floor. There were belts and buckles, and brown tags bearing names and dates. One battered case was covered in luggage labels, with places Ru had never even heard of. *Constantinople. Calcutta. Madras.*

'Wow.' Ru whistled. 'Whoever sets up the Ritzy Rails is serious about accuracy.'

'Oh, aren't they just?' Elfie swooned, caressing a feather boa with her cheek.

The next bag was a mahogany leather case similar to an old-fashioned doctor's kit. Its weight took Ru by surprise as she swung it on to the floor with a heavy *thud*.

'*Sssh*.' Malik glanced at the door, alarmed. 'I don't want him to hear us.'

'But we're not doing anything wrong,' Ru said, reaching towards the next cabinet. 'As long as we don't touch the flowers or leave the carriage, we're fine. Everything's at our disposal, remember?'

Malik swallowed and turned his head away.

'I think this one's locked.' Ru rattled the round knob, turning it this way and that way. It remained steadfastly closed. 'Why do you think it's—?'

Scrrritch. Scraatch.

Ru yelped and fell backwards off the chair.

Something was inside the cabinet. And it was trying to claw its way out.

FIFTEEN

'What on earth's in there?' Ru pointed upwards in disbelief. 'It's alive!'

'What?' Malik sat bolt upright, a dark cloud passing across his face. 'What is it?'

'Listen!' Ru put her fingers to her lips. It was still there.

Scrrritch. Scraatch.

Elfie's forehead wrinkled. 'Really? Let me listen.' She removed the feather boa from round her neck and joined Ru on the chair. 'Hmm. I can definitely hear something.' She stuck her tongue between her teeth and gripped the doorknob, her fingers turning white as she pulled. 'No good,' she panted, and released the handle. 'Stuck tight. But I think we've scared whatever was there, anyway. It's gone quiet.'

'Oh.' Malik sounded oddly sad as he slumped back into his seat. 'Has it?'

'Yeah.' Ru climbed back down, trying to resist glancing back at the locked cabinet. Elfie was right. The scratching noise had gone. So why were the hairs on the back of her neck still defiantly tingly? 'It must've been something outside. It's pretty windy out. Just a tree branch scratching the roof, I guess.'

Or maybe her nerves were so frayed she was imagining things. Maybe the tiredness was catching up with her. Maybe.

Eager to forget it, she lowered herself to the floor and crossed her legs. 'Remember, we're looking for anything we can use to write the note. It just needs to be small enough that we can slip it under the door without him seeing.'

Elfie and Ru split the cases between them, each labelled with strangers' names. *D. Elliot*, *A. Stokes*, *G. Thomas*, *M. Cheesley*. The coach fell into busy silence, and it was a relief to focus on something other than the red moon that never dimmed. Just how long was a lunar eclipse supposed to last anyway?

'Everything's so detailed.' Ru stroked the soft leather of the brown bag, warm to the touch. 'It feels real. I wonder if they do this on every Ritzy Rails service.' It was neatly packed with black lace-up shoes, a tweed cap, folded cloth pyjamas and a wooden comb, and tucked neatly at the bottom was a squat tin can. She lifted it out to take a closer look.

Déjà vu hit her like a freight train. She'd seen this before. Or one exactly like it at least, in the old Melbridge museum.

Rolled Ox Tongue.

Wasn't like she'd forget that in a hurry.

'Huh,' she muttered. She felt the weight of it in her hands. It definitely wasn't empty – not that she'd open it for a million quid – and the white label looked fresh and new.

But it was just a coincidence. Or maybe Ritzy Rails had used Melbridge's ghost station as inspiration. *Yes*, Ru decided satisfactorily. *That must be it.*

'Doesn't look like there's anything to write a note with.' Malik was peering over Elfie's shoulder from his chair. 'Sorry, Ruby.'

'Yep, no luck.' Elfie discarded one suitcase and went for the other. 'Only more costumes. Ooh, there's a *gorgeous* hat in here, though...'

The next suitcase was bulging at the seams,

with straining straps that looked fit to burst. Ru unbuckled them and the case popped open like a jack-in-the-box.

Inside, carefully folded, was a velvet cloak of deep forest colours and trimmed with yellow fabric flowers: marigolds, primroses, buttercups and others Ru didn't know the name of. Leaves of every green shade were pinned, cascading like a waterfall.

'Oh, *look* at it.' Elfie peered over Ru's shoulder. 'It's the most stunning thing I've ever seen. There's something tucked in the folds.' She pulled out what looked like a mask; also green, and edged with more fabric petals. Painted runes and twists of leaves circled the eyes. 'Cor, I think this is a Green Man costume. It's the best I've ever seen.'

Malik turned his head back to the window. His hands had clenched, and the fists rested on his thighs.

The mask glared at Ru with empty eye sockets and a large, mocking smile. It looked both ancient and modern at once, like a demon from one of Sam's old folk horror movies.

'Malik said the Green Man was strange.' Ru wriggled away from it. 'I don't like it. He's sinister.'

'Ru, no, he's not sinister at all! He's the spirit of rebirth.' Obviously awestruck, Elfie ran her hand over the leafy cloak. 'My mums say that all the old beliefs get told wrong. The Green Man figure is everywhere – on churches, old buildings . . . he chases away the winter darkness and brings forth the spring.'

'What's he doing on a steam train then?'

'It's May Eve, Ru,' Elfie explained patiently. 'The Green Man parades around in festivals and celebrations on May Day, especially round here. Some Wiltshire villages are still majorly into it all. It's one of the reasons we came down now, and I even learnt how to morris-dance and *everything*.'

Ru's brain sparked like a lit match. Cribbins and the Green Man costume felt connected somehow – as if their images were overlapping each other, back and forth. It was like the old trick Dad used to pull out at Christmas. An empty cage and a bird were drawn on either side of a paper circle, with string threaded through the middle. When Dad twirled the string, the circle would spin, blurring the images together, and *hey presto* the bird was trapped behind cage bars.

Only an illusion, of course. But it looked real.

So did the vision of Cribbins bent double in an ancient costume, draped in dead, mildewy leaves. His wide, mocking smile.

'I don't like it,' she said again.

'Well, I do,' Elfie murmured, half under her breath. 'Magic's more real than everyone thinks.'

Ru bit her tongue.

The two of them lifted the cases back into the cabinets, and Ru hoped the silence would be enough to end the conversation. All the paranormal stuff was making her itch with discomfort.

'We still haven't figured out how to alert the other passengers.' She plonked back on to the chair. 'Any ideas?'

'We could risk it and shout?' Elfie suggested.

'Cribbins would love that.' Ru chewed her lip and thought for a moment. The skin was as rough and chapped as chalk.

Chapped?

A long shot, but it was all they had.

'Elfie, your sister's lip balm. It's a stick, right? And cherry flavour? Red?'

'That's right.' Elfie looked wary. 'Why?'

Bingo.

Ru's expression must have given her away, because Elfie groaned and folded like damp cardboard.

'Eleanor will kill me if anything happens to it, Ru, it's Sephora, and all right, I nicked it off her, but . . .'

'We've been kidnapped, Elfie.' Ru held out her hand. 'I'm sure she'll let you off.'

SIXTEEN

Shadow-soaked fields sped past, blurry with smoke. *The Green Lady* was getting deeper and deeper into the middle of nowhere.

The two girls clustered around one table, both swaying slightly with the train. Elfie – having insisted that only *she* could use the lip balm – was pressing it lightly on her train ticket.

HLP

'Will that do?' She bit her thumbnail nervously.

'Um . . .' Ru scrabbled for something inoffensive. 'Great, but can you maybe write a bit more? Not sure they'll get that.'

Elfie put her rainbow head in her hands. 'I am *so* dead.' But she took the lip balm and wrote again:

> HELP! TRAPPED IN COACH C
> CALL 999 CONDUCTOR BAD

Just as Elfie lifted the squashed tip of the lip balm from the ticket, a gust of music floated through the carriage like a ghost.

Winter time has gone and past-o
Summer time has come at last-o
We shall sing and dance the day ...

'The song's started.' Malik's outline glowed crimson at the window. 'I . . . I don't think you should pass the note through yet.'

'It's now or never, Malik,' Ru said shortly. The distance from home was getting more painful by the minute. 'We can't wait.'

The sweet cherry scent on top of the bitter smoke pumping from the train's chimney crept into Ru's nostrils and made her stomach whirl. She pinched her nose, holding the ticket at arm's length.

'Listen, Ruby.' Malik leant cautiously to the edge of the seat. 'I'm really not sure now's the right time, he'll be here soon, I can't bear it ...'

'Malik, please, we don't know how long until the next stop. We have to do it now. I get it – it sucks Cribbins got cross with you, but we're getting help—'

'But you don't underst—'

Before her frustration could turn into a retort, Ru rapped on the door with her knuckles three times. 'We've got to get their attention.'

And come followin' the Green Man that brings the May...

Stamp, stamp, clap, laugh, violin, clap.

Ru knocked a few more times, but it was pointless. They weren't going to hear her through the racket. She knelt and peered through the thin gap in the door.

Outlines of legs danced behind it. She could see laced-up shoes twirling and sweeping the floor, and bouncing cuffs of frayed trousers. Scrunching one eye closed in concentration, she started to push the ticket through.

The whistle bellowed. Ru jumped, and the ticket became stuck beneath the thick carriage door.

'No, it's jammed!' She tried sliding it forward again, but it was caught by something unseen. 'I'm too clumsy for this – can someone else try?'

Elfie lowered her camera on to the empty seat next to Malik. 'I'll do it. Can you look after this, Malik?' She rushed over and stuck her fingers underneath the door.

He looked at the camera in alarm and budged closer to the window. 'But there's no time . . . the song . . . and the whistle . . .'

'He won't come, Malik, he said he's busy,' Ru hissed, too anxious to soften her edges. 'How are you getting on, Elfie?'

'I think it hit a nail or something. Just give me a minute . . . nearly there . . .'

Ru felt a judder and the unmistakable drag of the train slowing its pace. And there was something else, beneath the squeal of the brakes.

Tick-tock, tick-tock.

It was growing louder with each second.

An alarm rang in Ru's head. 'How's it going?'

'Almost . . .'

A-WOOO. The whistle screamed again, and floods of steam cascaded past the window.

Chuff-chuff. Tick-tock.

'He's here!' Malik yelled. 'Get back!'

And then more sounds. A jangle of keys. A deliberate, firm footstep. The unmistakable *clank* of a lock being turned.

Elfie and Ru flung themselves on to an armchair, landing on the cushion just as the door swung open.

SEVENTEEN

'I must apologize for the slight bump we experienced near Silbury Hill earlier. The wind is picking up, and fallen leaves rendered the tracks slippery. All done with now.' Cribbins stepped from the shadows into the oil lamps' warm glow. He held an elaborate silver tray in front of him.

Ru stifled a gasp. He looked different.

No, different was an understatement. Maybe Malik was right to be terrified.

The Conductor's skin was pale and sickly-looking, and the edges of his moustache were ragged, like he'd hacked at them with blunt scissors. There was a small tear in his jacket, just below the elbow, and dirty cream fabric poked through.

But by far the strangest thing was his expression.

His glass-blue eyes were unblinking, and an unnaturally wide smile was pasted on his waxen face, as if somebody had hooked the corners of his lips and pulled them tight.

Just like the Green Man mask.

A hand reached for hers. Elfie was trembling.

'More refreshments are in order.' His voice sounded lower than it had been. Less clipped, too, with the growling 'r' of old Wiltshire. 'As I promised. Everything you could possibly need.'

He lowered the tray on to the nearest table. A towering plate of fondant fancies and two steaming china cups sat in front of them. A single cup handle was a fraction off-centre, and with a *mmm hmm* he turned it so the cups were a precise, identical duo.

'Perfect.' He lifted his hat in farewell and spun back towards the door. To Ru's horror, she spied the creased note in his path. Cribbins must have trodden it in. To her eyes it burnt bright as a flare. Impossible to miss.

'Wait!' she yelled, not knowing what else to do. 'Stop!'

The Conductor paused. He turned his oily brown head – messier than before, tousled and peppered with something that looked like dust – over his shoulder. 'How may I help you, miss?'

'Why . . .' Ignoring Elfie's nails digging into her palm, she forced herself to stand. 'Why are you keeping us locked in here?'

She stood her ground as Cribbins slowly pivoted to face her, his wide-eyed expression unchanging. 'You look rather flushed, miss. And you appear to be out of breath. You're not sickening for something, are you?'

Ru's eyes flicked to the ticket again. She didn't know what would happen if he found it, or what he would do to them. But she knew it wouldn't be good.

Don't look down, she begged silently. *Don't look down.*

'No.' She sounded braver than she felt. 'You said we wouldn't see you for a while. Is this the final stop? Where are you taking us? And why are we locked in here?'

Something emerged in the distant dark. A station sign.

Cribbins tilted his head, fox-like. 'No, miss. We are not approaching the final stop. Rest assured, you will know when we are.' He gestured at the cups. 'Now please drink.'

Ru's blood simmered and boiled – from fear, or anger, or both, she didn't know – but Elfie's cool fingers wrapped around her wrist and tugged as if to say: *Don't*.

'Thank you,' she managed, and raised the cup to her lips.

Apparently satisfied, the Conductor nodded, pulled out his pocket watch and stared into its face. 'My, my,' he murmured, entranced. 'How time flies. We're almost at Devizes.'

Ru's heart gave a painful jolt. *Devizes already?* She'd never been that far from home without her family. She was driftwood, floating further and further from shore.

Cribbins returned the watch to his pocket. 'Do you know the Devizes Moonraker legend, miss?'

'No,' she replied through gritted teeth.

'They say that smugglers hid their stolen treasure in a local pond. When they came to retrieve it by nightfall and were accosted by local law men, they claimed to be "raking the cheese" in the pond, which was of course the moon's reflection.'

He backed towards the door, not once looking away from Ru.

No mention of the note. Ru held her breath.

Have we got away with it?

'The law men dismissed them as yokels and let them be.' Cribbins halted as the heel of his shoe crossed the doorway. 'The moral of the story? Never underestimate a Wiltshire man.' Without breaking Ru's gaze, he pointed to the floor. 'Whose ticket is this?'

No.

Panic filled Ru, heavy as iron. What would he do? It could be fine. It might be fine.

Cribbins lifted his trousers and crouched on the floor. His sock was crumpled and grubby at his ankle. 'Perhaps it's yours, Malik?'

Malik looked like he was about to be sick. The Conductor lifted the ticket, held it between two fingers and regarded it thoughtfully. His eerie smile faded.

Blood thrummed in Ru's ears.

Please don't look at the back. Please don't look at the back.

He flipped the ticket round. Elfie's hand was

sweaty on hers.

'A-ha,' said Cribbins. A two-syllable song.

Malik buried his head in his hands. Ru gripped Elfie and braced herself for whatever was coming next. What would he do to them? Covert communication never went well in TV shows. Their kidnapper always found them out and made them pay.

'Cherries?' Cribbins gave the ticket a neat little sniff. 'This must belong to you, Miss Midwinter.' He leant across Ru. The back of the ticket was facing upwards, and it gave Ru the slightest crumb of relief to see that the lip balm had smudged beyond recognition. All the words were smooshed together in a red gloopy mess.

Elfie took the ticket from him with shaking hands. 'Thanks,' she whispered. 'I... must've dropped it. Butterfingers.'

The strange beam returned to his face. 'We all make mistakes, Miss Midwinter,' he said. 'Some more than most. Perhaps that is precisely what brings us all here tonight.' Cribbins' eyes fell on Ru.

Tick-tock, tick-tock. It bore into her skull.

'Don't you think, Miss Darke? Or should I say Miss Cole?'

EIGHTEEN

After he'd left, the whistle moaned again. But nobody else made a sound.

Ru stared outside until the fear was quelled, trying to weigh down the thoughts that flew like paper caught by the wind.

Why did he call her Cole? How on earth had he known her mum's family name?

She'd just gaped at him, unable to answer.

Her senses were overloaded, which was never a good sign. The dark, oppressive night, stars blazing out from behind the steam, the fiery blood moon, unnaturally large, the wild mass of bramble hedges bent sideways with the wind, the jig from the next carriage, the train's insistent *chug* slowing as it approached the oncoming station – each fighting for space in her head. The landslide was growing threateningly close. Automatically, she reached out, longing for the calm safety of Mum and Dad.

But they weren't there. So she just wouldn't think about any of it. No other option. She hugged herself tightly.

'He looks ill.' Malik was staring at his own reflection in the window, brushing his hair across his forehead furtively. 'Or wounded.'

'Maybe he's been attacked,' Ru said, only half-joking. 'Maybe someone's fighting for us.'

'Unfortunately, I doubt that.' Elfie sat cross-legged, twirling multicoloured strands of hair between her fingers. 'But something's definitely changed with him. The question is, what? And how?'

Ru turned back to the window. She didn't want to think about that either.

Devizes station was more built up than the others, with two signal posts towering over multiple sets of train tracks that spread out like the veins of a leaf. A ticket office, a waiting room and a quaint café extended from the enclosed platform, with white pillars, wooden doors, and tunnelled stairs that crossed over the tracks and down to the other side.

Victorian lamps edged out through the pink-tinted smoke.

The Green Lady glided past at a pace only slightly faster than walking, and in one dizzy moment, Ru thought that the train might stop, that Cribbins had had a change of heart, but no; as they reached the end of the platform the whistle bellowed again, and the *chuff-chuff* doubled its speed. She could only watch as the black-and-white sign disappeared from her eyeline.

Devizes.

A familiar place in a horribly unfamiliar situation.

Dad had taken her and Sam to the market in Devizes a few times, to search for vintage board games. They'd munch their well-earned cakes in the car on the way back, which was odd now she came to think of it, because Dad usually took them on the train on his outings. '*So I can hang out with you,*' he'd grin.

But he had to drive, he'd always said, because there wasn't a station in Devizes.

A prickle itched the back of her skull. Gram had mentioned something. What was it?

Devizes . . . Holt . . . Broughton Gifford Halt . . .

nearly all the station buildings are gone.

She twisted round on her chair, watching the station buildings – which were absolutely, definitely there – swan further backwards into the distance. The sign was the last thing to vanish into the smoke.

Devizes.

Oh.

She was hit by a stab of terror. Nothing about this was right.

'We have to go. We have to get out of here. Now.' She leapt to her feet and darted to the door. She went to rattle the handle, to yank it with all of her strength, but even without touching it she could feel the heat radiating from the metal. She held back, determined to quash the sly whisper in her head.

It's him. He makes the handle burn and it cools when he leaves. This isn't normal, Ru. You know that.

She shook it away.

'The music's gone quieter again,' Elfie said. 'In the next carriage.'

'They'll hear me now, then.' Ru knocked three times, sharp and short.

No answer. She put her ear to the door. No sound at all. Only the train's exhale.

'They shouldn't be *that* quiet.' She knelt down and peered through the gap.

There was nothing there. Just tree shadows sliding along the walls. No dancing legs. No stamping. No people. The corridor was totally empty.

'What? Where is everyone?'

Elfie's head squashed next to hers, and rainbow hair tickled Ru's nose. 'Oh my days. They've all gone.'

'Everybody?' gulped Malik. 'They've all gone? Where did they go?'

Ru's pulse accelerated. 'I don't know. But there's nobody. It's just us.'

She'd felt alone before, especially over the last few months. Multiple wide-awake nights, staring at the ceiling. Mum and Dad breaking the news. Parties, when everyone else had both parents by their side. Whole families at school concerts.

But this was different. It wasn't just that they were alone. They were trapped. Buried by night, racing away from everything they knew and totally without help.

Ru got to her feet and finally allowed herself to look at Elfie. A heavy, knowing gaze met hers. She'd seen that gaze before, when Gram had insisted on reading Mum's tarot cards before the split. She'd known then. She'd known before any of them.

'I can still fix this, Elfie,' Ru promised, fists clenched at her side. 'I'm going to figure out a plan.'

Elfie looked at her for a long time. 'Of course you will, Ru. But we're going to figure it out together. You're not fixing this alone, OK?'

To her embarrassment, Ru felt spiky tears scraping at her eyes. 'OK,' she said huskily. 'Together.'

NINETEEN

Ru breathed on the window, and a misty cloud spread across the glass. If they had any chance of getting out of there, they needed a plan. Which meant she had to remember the stations Gram had pointed out.

But what if you can't? Doubt hissed in her ear.

Her memory was usually as sharp as a diamond, but now it was fuzzy with fear and she could only conjure up the blurriest images of her notes and the old station map. Taking a deep breath, she scribbled station names in the condensation until she reached the end of the glass, then stepped back like a painter surveying her work. 'That's all I can remember. I'm sorry.'

Elfie snapped multiple shots with her camera,

then hurriedly scrubbed the glass clean with her sleeve. 'It's more than enough. Your memory's amazing, Ru.'

'Guess there are some benefits to my messily wired brain.' Ru bent over the camera screen. She'd clearly fudged some names, but she'd remembered more places than she'd thought. That gave her a small pinch of pride.

'Malik?' She glanced at the boy, still in his chair. He'd curved himself away from them at a strange angle. 'Do you want to take a look at the stations?'

'No,' Malik replied. 'I'm all right over here.'

'It's OK, I'll bring the camera to—'

'No!' he snapped.

Ru backed away, hands up, palms out. 'Oh, OK. Sure.' She pulled a face at Elfie. A soundless question.

'He just needs space for a minute, Ru, that's all.' Elfie's hand was on her wrist again. 'Hey listen, I think I'm on to something. There's something really significant about the stations you've listed.'

'Elfie, as much as I love your facts, we don't have time...'

'No, no, listen – this is part of it, I *swear*,' Elfie protested shrilly. 'I *knew* the stations we passed reminded me of something. I got on at Ogbourne, you got on at Avebury . . . and as well as those two, you wrote down a bunch of CRAZY-important places.' She ran her finger along the camera screen. 'Oh, and you put *West Sockton*, but that's probably *West Penstick*, which happens to be right next to Glastonbury. Ta-da!' She clapped her hands and held her arms out as if expecting applause.

'And that means . . . what?' Ru asked, lost.

'Everything!' Elfie exploded. 'On one single railway line, there are all these places of extreme mystical energy. There are so many I can't even mention them all . . . Royston Caves, Silbury Hill, Avebury, even Glastonbury Tor! Look, I've got that on my boot!'

She lifted her foot and stamped it down on to the chair, prodding at the curled symbols she'd drawn. 'This seven-coiled spiral represents Glastonbury Tor. That place is a total legend in mythology, and sits *smack-bang* atop a world-famous magical current that sweeps across the country – the Michael Line – which we just so happen to be riding on!' Elfie's breath ran short, her cheeks turning puce. 'The Tor is this epically awesome beacon of earth magic and mystical energy, and so it'll be the final stop Cribbins promised, for whatever diabolical plan he has in mind, I'm sure of it!' She finally ran out of air with a ragged wheeze.

'Oooh.' Ru tried to sound a little bit enthusiastic for Elfie's sake. 'Ley lines. Yeah, Gram said they built the MWL where they imagined one was, or something.'

'Of course they did.' Elfie swept ethereally to the window, lightly pressing both palms on the glass. 'It explains everything. And there's a lunar eclipse – tonight, on May Eve. This is a night when . . .'

'. . . when tricksters, spirits and demons can wander the earth,' Ru said flatly. 'I've heard.'

'Oh, come on,' Elfie sighed. 'You know as well as I do that something weird is going on. Are you *honestly* telling me Cribbins is a . . .' She lowered her voice to a whisper. 'Regular conductor? Listen to your gut, Ru. Tricksters, spirits and demons. You can't keep ignoring the obvious.'

Ice crept up Ru's spine and spread through her veins until she was freezing cold. 'I . . . I just . . .'

Everything in her was battling the unease that had begun the moment she'd set eyes on *The Green*

Lady: the disembodied voices, the music, the burnt hand, the *scriiitch scraaatch*, and worst of all, the inhuman look in Cribbins' eyes.

Or should I say Miss Cole?

Was he everything Gram had warned her about?

No. Ru was her father's daughter. *Logic versus emotions.*

'Well, we don't need to think about any of that,' she said. 'We just need to figure a way out.'

Challenge: Get us out of The Green Lady. Go.

Pretending she couldn't see the hurt that flittered across Elfie's face, Ru pored over the stations she'd listed. Her brain whirred. 'Does anyone know how fast steam trains go?'

'Um . . .' Malik raised a tentative hand. 'Forty to fifty miles per hour on average for a passenger locomotive. When it slows down near the stations, perhaps fifteen or twenty miles per hour. Why?'

'Well, according to this . . .' Ru zoomed in on the picture. 'We've got Trowbridge next. Trowbridge is a busy town, even at night. Loads of people live there. So I'd say we aim for that.'

'Aim?' Malik shrank back. 'What do you mean, aim?'

Elfie caught on quickly. 'Hang on . . . are you saying what I think you're saying?'

'I might well be.'

'What is she saying?' Malik squeaked. 'What's happening?'

'But all the doors are locked, inside and outside.' Even as Elfie spoke, a glimmer of excitement lit up her face. Fear, too. 'Even if it does go slow enough to be safe, how would we get out?'

Ru tapped on the window with her knuckles. Her suspicions were right.

'These old windows are made with much thinner glass than trains today. So we'll smash one, and then we'll jump out. OK?'

Twenty

Elfie made a noise that sounded like a cross between a giggle and a whimper. 'Smash a window. Jump while the train's still moving. Escape.'

'It should be easy enough,' Ru said encouragingly. 'If it's as slow as Malik says, all we need to do is tuck and roll, and we'll be fine, won't we Malik?'

'In . . . in theory,' he rasped, and then didn't say any more.

Doubt rose like steam. In perfect unison, Malik and Elfie turned their eyes to the landscape outside, and Ru knew exactly what they were thinking, because she was thinking it too.

The Green Lady ran slower than a car, yes, but the untamed countryside was still a mystery. Would it kill them, jumping out? What if they landed on stone, instead of grass? Even worse – what if they landed on the tracks? How could Ru do that 'tuck and roll' thing she'd seen in films when she could barely walk in a straight line without tripping over her feet?

But they didn't have any other choice, did they?

'There's no other way. None at all.' Ru cracked her sore knuckles. 'Look, we all know we've got to get out of here before that final stop. Who knows what Cribbins has got planned for us? We'll just . . . we'll aim for a soft landing.'

'Hmm.' Elfie gnawed anxiously on a fondant fancy. 'Say we did jump. We could nab some of the costumes from the suitcases, maybe, and pad ourselves up? I don't fancy breaking any bones.'

'Yes! Great idea!' Ru climbed on to the seat and threw open the first two cabinets. She chucked the luggage down to Malik's table, and it landed with a *thunk.* He flinched, but still didn't move.

The locked cabinet loomed large, and Ru eyed it warily.

Scriiitch-scraaatch.

It was back. The sound sent a shiver through her skin and down to her bones.

'Um, there's . . .' She stopped herself. They were about to get off anyway. She filed it in the *not going to think about it* box – which was getting fuller by the second – and started the climb back down.

The train swung sharply around a corner, and Ru fell on to the table with a *smack*. The vase spun and tumbled off the table, sending the purple and white blossoms flying on to the floor. Water pooled into a dark stain on the carpet.

'Pick it up!' Malik was kneeling on the chair, limbs rigid. 'Don't touch the flowers, he said don't touch the flowers, please don't touch the flowers!'

'All right, Malik, it was just an accident.' Red-faced and flustered, Ru gathered up the mess and put the vase back on the table. 'See? All fine.'

'The bluebell's bent!' Malik pointed hysterically. 'Straighten it quickly, before he notices!'

Elfie was watching him intently. 'Malik, are you OK?' She edged gingerly towards him. 'You look poorly all of a sudden.'

'I . . .' He pulled further away from her, and wiped his palm across his forehead. 'I do feel a little unwell . . .'

Ru swiped the bent bluebell and stuffed it into

her pocket. The vase was perfect once more. Well, almost. Nearly. Close enough. 'See? He'll never know.'

Malik nodded absently and sank back into his seat. 'Good. Thank you.' He seemed infinitely lighter, as if a stone had lifted from his chest. 'Ruby, I'm so sorry I shouted at you. That wasn't fair.'

'Forget it. I've heard way worse from my brother. Now let's grab what we can out of the suitcases, quickly, before he comes back. And layer up.'

She shook off her denim jacket and hurriedly put on too-big pyjamas, a cloth cap that barely fit with her beret and mass of hair, a knitted vest, and several pairs of socks. She squeezed her denim jacket over them, the buttons stretched to their limit. She was bulged and lumpy, like a full sack of coal.

Elfie chose two cloth dresses and a wool cardigan, and stuffed them under her velvet coat. 'Ohhh, I wish I could take these!' she gushed, pulling some shoes out of a case. 'Proper vintage high heels, I think – *look* at them.'

Ru grinned sardonically. 'Not sure high heels are the best . . .' Ru's words died in her throat as Elfie held up the heels. They were gold leather, adorned with a dainty bow. They were also strikingly similar to the torn shoe she'd seen at the Melbridge museum.

Identical, even.

'Er, yeah. Ha,' Ru laughed weakly. Her hands and forehead were clammy with sweat. 'Probably not good for escaping.'

They're not identical. It's a coincidence. Don't be an idiot.

Why couldn't she stop trembling?

'Hey, Malik,' Elfie called gently. 'Aren't you going to choose some padding?'

'No.' He spoke barely above a whisper, not looking at either of them. 'But I . . . I have noticed something that may be of help.'

'Go on.' Ru placed the suitcases back in the cabinets and ignored her shaking hands.

'Cribbins is a very fastidious man. That is, he appears to be.'

'Fastidy-whatty?'

'I mean, I believe he . . . he likes things just so,' Malik explained. 'The flowers and vases, for example, and no other railway employee looks as neatly pressed and starched as he does.' He frowned. 'And see – the cups had to be in a perfect position. Not to mention how the pink cakes are arranged, all stacked like the bricks of a wall. Nobody else from the Mid Wessex Line arranges them like that. Only him.'

Ru took one from the bottom and watched the rest fall. *Take that, Cribbins.* Her own small, spiteful rebellion.

'Do you know a lot of people from the MWL then, Malik?' she asked curiously. 'It's the first time you've mentioned that.'

'A . . . a few.' He pressed himself against the window, as far back as he could go. 'Anyway, things happen in a certain order when he appears in this coach. There's a . . . sequence which is always the same. Like clockwork.'

'What do you mean?'

'It starts with the music. And the train begins to slow. Then the whistle blows. Then the Conductor appears for a short while, then leaves. And then the whistle blows again.'

Ru rewound the journey in her head. To her amazement, Malik was right. Always in the exact same order. 'Get you,' she said, admiringly. 'I hadn't noticed that. Ten points to Malik Marley.'

Malik looked faintly pleased. 'He likes things how

he likes them, but that means it's a weakness too. Predictability, for one.'

Likes things how he likes them, Ru thought, with a pang. *That's what Sam said about me.*

No, she was nothing like Cribbins.

'It's almost like a ritual,' Elfie said, through another mouthful of cake. 'And rituals are so revealing. We've all got stuff we do in a particular order, just cos it makes us feel safe. Like, I always have to say goodnight to our beech tree before bed, then eat a crumpet, but NEVER the other way round. See, rituals aren't just for witchcraft – they're like secret clues to who we are and what makes us tick.' She swallowed the cake and grinned. 'Or in Cribbins' case, tick-tock.'

'I pick my mum a daisy,' Malik murmured. Ru hadn't noticed before how painfully small he was. His waistcoat looked like a younger child's size, the buttons glinting bronze in the lamplight. One was missing, the thread ripped. Had it always been like that? 'I pick a daisy every morning from our garden. Then I leave it by her ... by her pillow. So she can see it when she wakes up.'

Ru longed for the safety of home and her own

little rituals. So much it hurt.

Feed Grizabella, eat toast, two chess moves with Dad, chat with Mum, get dressed, meet Abeni at bus stop.

Whether or not she was getting off this train, things were never going back to how they were. She stuffed that feeling in a box, too.

'Why *doesn't* Cribbins stay in the coach for very long?' she frowned. 'If I'd kidnapped someone, I wouldn't want to risk them escaping. I wouldn't let them out of my . . .'

Winter time has gone and past-o

Music flooded the carriage. Beset with adrenaline and fear, Ru wrapped her arms around the bumpiest sections of clothes.

'Cover up. Don't let him see the padding. He'll be here any second.'

TWENTY-ONE

They hugged themselves and waited for the tell-tale sounds of Cribbins' approach.

'Once he leaves,' Ru whispered, 'we wait until the whistle blows again, then we smash the glass.'

'What with?' Elfie matched her volume. 'Dunno about you, but I've left my battering ram at home.'

'Um . . .' Ru looked around the carriage. 'It's thin glass. We'll just bash it with everything we can. Our elbows, the vases, your boots, Elfie . . .'

'So we smash the glass,' Elfie repeated slowly, 'then jump out, tuck and roll, and then . . . ?'

'Run for our lives?' Ru tried to give her a smile. 'There's a taxi rank at Trowbridge station. We'll jump in a taxi and get as far away as possible.'

She threw a look towards Malik, his small frame

almost swallowed by the chair he'd refused to leave. His eyes were fixed to the door, looking even more petrified than she felt. What did he know that they didn't?

The whistle wailed like a ghostly call into the night. The moment it died, one of the lamps fizzed and flickered, then burst into a shower of splintered glass.

Tick-tock. Tick-tock.

Ru's blood froze. It was coming from inside the carriage.

Grasping wildly for each other's hands, Ru and Elfie lifted their heads to see Cribbins striding towards them, swinging his pocket watch like a pendulum.

'Tick-tock.' He smiled. 'How time flies.'

Ru's hands flew to her mouth in horror. He'd looked wrecked the last time. But that had been nothing.

Now his pristine jacket was a mass of tangled threads barely held together, and on his white shirt a dark stain bloomed. Half of his face was cast in the shadow of an oil lamp, the other half chequered with glistening cuts and bruises. His mouth, however, was still preserved in the same strange, twisted smile.

What's happened to him?

He wound the pocket watch chain and dropped it into his torn pocket, scanning the carriage with suspicious eyes. Fresh sweat glistened in streams on his grey skin. 'Something's amiss in here.'

Ru and Elfie exchanged panicked looks and tried to slink further behind the table.

Please don't notice the clothes, Ru begged silently. *Don't.*

'A vase has been tampered with.'

What? She'd forgotten all about the spillage. But the water had dried quickly, and the broken bluebell was in her back pocket. How could he tell?

The Conductor drew in a jagged breath, his teeth bared. It was the warning sound of an animal about to strike. Slowly, he swept down the aisle, past Ru and Elfie, then Malik. Malik's eyes closed as Cribbins passed, his fingers crossed.

Cribbins stopped at the table where Ru had fallen and fixed his eagle-eyes at the vase. 'I do not like repeating myself.'

He spoke with a threatening quiet, as dark and

slippery as oil. 'And this will be the last time I do so. You *do not* touch the vase or its contents. Do I make myself clear?'

Three nods. Ru's mind was a block of ice.

'I am disappointed.' Cribbins still had his back to them, his voice ominously low. 'You have not enjoyed your refreshments.'

Wind smacked the glass. Ru's sense of foreboding grew heavier.

'No, no, we loved . . .' she began hastily, but his hand flew up to silence her.

'That was not a question.' He turned his head, and for a few awful seconds, Ru could've sworn it swivelled all the way round, his gaze as piercing as a hunting owl's. But when she blinked, his body was just as it should be.

The unnatural smile spread across his face again, like a twisting snake. 'If you'd enjoyed them so much, you would be happier. Drink your cocoa. Eat your cakes. Coach C has everything your heart could desire.'

'But . . .'

'Listen, you arrogant swine!' Cribbins roared. Two more oil lamps shattered, and he glided through the glass on the floor.

To Ru's utter horror, he made his way to her and crouched to her height, so their faces were nearly touching. His glass-like eyes locked on to hers.

Ru couldn't breathe. Elfie was frozen at her side.

'Have you forgotten how you failed everybody?' Cribbins seethed, and his breath stank like decay. 'You're nothing but a reckless, swaggering failure. And now you follow *me* for once. Do as I say.'

Ru stared at him, too scared to move. His stinging words rang painfully true – because she had failed, hadn't she? – but she had the strangest feeling it wasn't her he was talking to.

Elfie nudged her in the ribs. 'Oh, we'd love to have the rest!' she trilled joyfully. 'Come on, Ru; I know we've been saving the fancies for the best moment, but I think this is it, don't you?' With a meaningful glint in her eye, she handed Ru her cup and a handful of cakes.

Ru nodded, and under the steel-cut gaze of Cribbins she tipped her head back and poured the lukewarm hot chocolate down her throat. It was probably delicious. But terror made it taste like seawater.

The Conductor's expression didn't alter. 'Now the cakes.'

Ru thought she might throw up. She squashed the fondant fancies until they became a mass of pink gloop and threw all of them into her mouth. Her stomach churned.

'All done.' Elfie swallowed with a shiver. She'd turned a worrying shade of white. 'Yum.'

'Best cakes ever,' Ru managed, two thumbs up. 'Thank you. Sir.'

A beat, then Cribbins leapt up and raised his hat. Patches of hair were missing from his head. Elfie squeaked and dug her nails into Ru's palm.

'Excellent,' he said lightly, back to his normal boyish way. 'You will be pleased to hear that dinner will be served shortly. Roast beef. See? Everything you could desire, here in Coach C.'

Ru held her breath as he swept away the crockery and headed into the corridor. It was the first time she'd been grateful to hear the door lock.

'It's over,' she said immediately. 'We are getting out of here.'

'You don't have to tell me twice.' Elfie grimaced. 'I'm a vegetarian. Apart from chocolate mousse.'

We shall sing and dance the day
And come followin' the Green Man that brings
the May . . .

Ru darted to the window and squinted into the darkness. The signal box slid past, the peeling *TROWBRIDGE* sign glinting in the crimson moonlight of the eclipse. Then it was gone, replaced by more vast, empty fields that stretched into hedge-bordered hills.

'OK . . .' She spoke faster than she could think, horribly aware of their chance slipping through her fingers. 'If the signal box is here, the station must be close by.'

Just as Malik had predicted, the whistle blew for a second time. The click of a stopwatch.

'Time to start smashing,' Ru ordered. '*Now.*'

TWENTY-TWO

Their costumes padded them perfectly. But even with multiple socks pulled up to her knees, and enough layers to survive the Arctic, Ru had never felt more breakable.

Jumping out of a moving train had *so* not been on her to-do list this morning. She couldn't think about anything other than the next few seconds – not about Mum, or Dad. Not about Sam, or Gram, or Grizabella, or her perfectly imperfect little life. There would be time for that.

'Elfie?' She climbed on to the chair behind Malik, who still hadn't moved. 'Can you . . . ?'

'My boots?' Elfie was already unlacing them, wearing a gleeful grin. 'On it.'

'I'll cover the glass to stop the spray.' Ru shook off

her denim jacket and held it up to the window. 'Wait!' Something caught her eye in the window's bottom corner. It was tiny. Likely never meant to be seen.

'Ru, we don't have time!' Elfie was poised with boot in hand, ready to strike.

'No, I know, but look.' She pointed at the blurred patch of breath. Inside it, scrawled in minute, almost-too-small-to-read writing – scratched by a fingernail perhaps – were the words:

I hate you.

Caught in the red light of the eclipse, it looked almost like it had been written in blood.

'Well, that's kind of creepy,' Elfie frowned. 'Who do you think wrote it?'

'Doesn't matter.' Ru shook off the pinpricks of fear snaking up her spine. 'You're right; we don't have time. Go!'

With an almighty grunt, Elfie launched her boot at the window. It bounced off and landed on the table.

'Don't worry!' Ru cried. 'Keep trying.'

Elfie cricked her neck, moved further back and threw the boot with all her might. It missed the window totally and flew instead towards the locked cabinet.

'Sorry!' she groaned.

Scrrritccch-scraaatch.

What happened next was too fast for Ru to register right away. The cabinet door flew open as the boot collided with it. Something howled, and a mass of black and grey hurled out of it, landing on the floor of the carriage with a graceful twist of its body.

With simultaneous shouts, Ru and Elfie threw themselves back on to their chairs in a huddle. The creature regarded them with a bright yellow stare, then licked a paw and yawned.

'Wait, is that . . . ?' Elfie stood and edged forward incredulously. 'Ru, that's a cat!'

Ru didn't move. She'd gone numb. *I know.*

'A cat.' Malik's small voice cut through the shadows. 'There was a cat in the cabinet?'

'*That* was the scratching?' Elfie said in disbelief. 'How is it still alive?'

I know that cat. I've seen that cat before. But not like this.

The cat sliced the air with its tail, and with a determined *mew*, it sprang off the floor and into Malik's lap, where it turned in a circle, pawed at his legs and snuggled down.

Malik's mouth fell open. 'Ned?' he whispered, and his expression flooded with recognition. He gave a small cry and stuck his head in the cat's fur. 'Oh, Ned. I missed you. How I missed you.'

As Ru watched them both with a dreadful realization, the music burst into life once more.

So, Hail! Hail! The First of May-o!
For it is the first summer's day-o!

A landslide was beckoning, blackening the edges of her brain like burnt paper. The violin strings, the layered sounds and smells, and the new revelations on top of each other, all clamouring to be noticed.

Not now. Shake it off, Ru.

Finally the *Trowbridge* sign emerged from the steam, followed by the long canopied platform and the shapes of the Victorian flats opposite. Mouth pressed in a grim line, she grabbed Elfie's boot.

'Protect your faces.' She thumped the glass with the boot's heel, again and again, repeatedly, until the faint cracking became as intense as the sound of a glacier collapsing into the sea. A gush of cold air poured into the stale carriage.

'No chance he didn't hear that.' Ru pulled the jacket from the window, which was now a jagged frame of glass. 'We have to get out now.'

Tick-tock. Tick-tock. Closer and closer.

'I can hear footsteps,' Malik warned. 'He's running.'

Ru took in the broken window and the approaching platform, the speeding strides getting louder and closer to their carriage. There was no time to waste.

'Elfie, you go first.'

She caught Elfie's fleeting, frightened look as she put her boot back on, then climbed on to the chair and perched on the edge of the window. 'I don't want to leave you, Ru . . .'

'I'll be right after you. Go!'

She bit her cheek so hard she could taste blood, and watched as Elfie jumped out, her rainbow hair flying behind her like wings. Elfie landed on a grass bank, her padded dress cushioning her fall. Her eyes were wide with shock, but she was alive.

Wobbly with relief, Ru held out her hand. 'Your turn, Malik.'

The boy looked down at the cat and pulled Ned closer to him. 'I'm not going.'

Metallic jangles and loud strides grew louder. Nearer.

'Malik, there's no time, *come on*!'

He leant wordlessly into the moonlight, revealing a gigantic bruise that covered his forehead and cheek, squeezing his eye shut. Was that new? 'Oh, Ruby. I can't leave. But you know that, don't you?'

And there it was. The clawing instinct she'd been steadfastly ignoring. How *off* he'd seemed. How he hadn't moved from his chair, not for a second. Station Ned. 'I . . . I think so. I'm so sorry, Malik.'

'Me too.' The ghost of a tear fell down his cheek. 'Now go. He's coming.'

Ru climbed up and on to the window ledge, the splintered glass slicing painfully into her skin.

The train was still going slow enough. She could do it. If Elfie could do it, so could she.

To her horror, the door lock *clinked*, followed by a low, unearthly growl. Without looking back she threw herself out of the window and prayed she'd land on something soft, too.

The wind was stronger than she'd anticipated. It snatched her and pulled her sideways, and she looked down just in time to see the grass hurtling up to meet her, and the sloping edge of the station platform.

Too late to tuck and roll, she threw herself awkwardly to the side so her head and shoulders landed on the grass, with only her leg skimming the platform.

'Ru!' Elfie screamed from a distance. 'Are you OK?'

She wanted to shout that it didn't hurt, it was just a graze, but she could only lie in the grass and try to catch her racing breath. She stared at the mass of stars and the blood-red moon that shone brighter than anything she'd ever seen.

They were out. They'd done it. She was free.

TWENTY-THREE

'We need to get out of here.' Elfie appeared above her, blocking out the moon. 'The train's stopping.'

Ru sat up with a wince. Pain shot through her leg, and to her dismay there was a long tear in her favourite cords. It had sliced through the two pairs of pyjama bottoms underneath.

Train brakes squealed like an animal being slaughtered, and the shape of a man in uniform glared from the slashed emptiness of the carriage window.

He was eerily still. In the red moonlight, pearly teeth glinted.

He was smiling.

That was somehow more terrifying than if he'd been roaring.

'Over the bank,' Ru whispered, rising to a crouch.

They linked hands, and, keeping low, they sneaked up the bank and slipped into the darkness of the ditch beyond. The wind howled above them, and their ragged breaths fell in time with each other. Ru's leg throbbed painfully, but she locked on to the feeling of Elfie's hand in hers, keeping each other safe.

'I tried to make Malik jump, honestly,' Ru whispered. 'But he wouldn't.'

Elfie sighed. She didn't look surprised. 'I know, Ru. I don't think he can, can he?'

Ru shook her head, and to her dismay tears finally forced their way out of her eyelids. She hurriedly wiped them with her grass-stained sleeve. 'But I don't want to talk about it. OK? Let's just not talk about it yet. Otherwise, it's all too . . .'

'Too real?' Elfie finished. 'Yeah. Not yet. But hey.' She bundled Ru into a tight hug. 'We're out. We're back home and away from that train, aren't we? We're all safe now.'

The Green Lady's whistle screamed, and vast plumes of smoke spread below them with the same bitter taste as Melbridge.

'Not yet we're not. We can't stay here; too

exposed.' She peered behind them, taken aback to see nothing but the swathes of inky fields. 'This . . . this can't be Trowbridge,' she frowned.

'I think it is,' Elfie whispered. 'Look.'

Ru peered over the bank to the station, tinged in red light. *The Green Lady* was skating to a stop across one of two lines that ran between the adjacent platforms. Both were covered by jagged canopies, with an enclosed walkway tunnel between them. It was too dark to see any more, but there was no mistaking the large brown and white sign stuck into the ground.

TROWBRIDGE.

'But . . . it's too empty, isn't it? Where's the car park, and the shops?'

'There are buildings over there.' Elfie pointed to the far end of the station, past the platform. In the dull light, Ru could just make out the pointed roofs of buildings, tall chimney chutes and the old pork pie factory, long since converted into flats.

'Oh, right,' she said, uncertain. 'Suppose we just came in a different side. The taxi rank must be further up there.'

'Do you think so?' Elfie murmured.

Ru didn't want to answer that.

Just as *The Green Lady* slithered beyond the station and out of sight, the squeal of brakes came to an abrupt halt.

'It's finally stopped.' Ru's heart plummeted. 'He's coming for us.' Boiling water *hissed* and smoke blanketed the night sky. 'We need to find some help at the station. Quick, while he's getting out and can't see us.'

'Wait, Ru!' Elfie yanked Ru's jacket as she stood. 'Let's take our chances in the fields. It's pitch black – he'll never see us out there.'

Ru smarted with frustration. 'Haven't you seen any horror movies, Elfie? We'd be helpless out there. We get to the taxi rank and we get help.'

She climbed out of the ditch and was almost knocked sideways by a powerful gust of wind.

'Ru, hold on, there might not be anyone there at all, cos it's night-time; it's safer out there in the fields, we'll end up at a farmhouse or something...'

'No!' Ru called over her shoulder as she skidded down the bank. 'That's a lot less safe, OK?'

The answering silence made her sting with guilt. But Ru could hear Elfie's feet behind her as she ran to the station building, and she was absolutely sure they'd made the right decision, especially when she saw a single light flickering through an open door.

The relief made her giddy. 'Someone's in there!'

They climbed towards the platform, pausing at the gate that barred the way. Somebody was talking. It was a man with a deep voice and a local accent, and he was mid-conversation. Ru couldn't make out everything he said, but it sounded like he was on the phone.

'... later with ... fog awful ... can't see nose ... face ...' There came a hearty laugh, a deep guffaw from the pits of his belly.

'Listen!' Ru squeaked. 'We're saved!'

She felt a tug at her coat. Elfie's face was screwed up in fear. 'Ru, hang on ...'

But Ru didn't want to. And she didn't want to hear any more of Elfie's doubts, either. She turned away and climbed over the gate. 'We can't stop. Cribbins will be on his way here any minute.'

Elfie's 'OK' was barely audible, but she leapt over the gate. Her boots landed on the platform with an echoing thud.

The man burst into peals of laughter again. Ru

couldn't wait to find a grown-up to take charge and worry about things, so they could stop panicking and go home. She darted through the open door and into the warmth of a room with the cheerful-sounding man and the glimmering light.

'Please, we need help—' she started, but the words died in her throat.

The light *was* on. But the room was empty.

There was nobody there.

Twenty-Four

'Where is he?' Ru frowned. 'He was in here. I heard him.'

There was no other way in or out of the office. Only the door they'd come through. A sign bearing STATIONMASTER was secured to it, in the same fashion as the Conductor's *MWL* insignia.

'Well, maybe he wasn't in here after all.' She swept back on to the platform, Elfie scurrying a few steps behind. Another door was open, and it cast a thin glow of light.

'Was that open before?' Elfie said. 'I don't think it was open before.'

Ru couldn't remember.

She stepped inside. It was a waiting room, filled with rows of unoccupied wooden chairs. The lower half of the wall was painted in solid green, and the upper in cream, adorned with framed watercolour paintings of steam trains. Vases of fresh bluebells and blossoms were placed in the four corners. Just like Coach C.

Further up the track, a train door slammed.

'Cribbins!' Ru ran to Elfie, who lingered at the door, looking pale.

'But Ru . . .'

A cheery voice cut her off, booming across the station. He sounded further away now. '. . . staff trip coming early . . . afore any passenger train, would you believe . . . all wearing antlers and paint . . .' More guffaws. 'Up at the Tor, later!'

'Where is he?' Ru dived out of the waiting room.

Two doors on the opposite platform were ajar.

'Over there!' Ru panted. She led them up a staircase, across the walkway and down the other side. 'Maybe he's on his mobile.'

She wasn't sure who she was trying to convince. Elfie, or herself.

'Ru . . .'

Ru ignored her, careering across the platform and through another door. A bell tinkled as she crashed it open.

She found herself in a quaint vintage café, with antique chairs and tables, cream pillars, and blackboards behind the counter that listed the menu in cursive chalk. Cakes, scones and tea loaves were displayed under glass, and steam bubbled from a boiling tea urn.

'So *someone* was here . . .' Ru's voice echoed under the high ceiling. 'They can't be far if they've just boiled the water.'

'Something's baking.' Elfie eyed her with an annoyingly meaningful look. 'It's vintage, wouldn't you say, Ru? Just like *The Green Lady*.'

No, no, no.

She wasn't going to hear it. There was no way she could even think about it.

'Maybe we've just wandered into a film set!' Ru's voice was helium-high. 'It's night-time; that's when these crews do filming isn't it, so they don't disturb people?'

'I don't know,' said Elfie.

'Well, they do,' said Ru, storming back on to the platform, leaving Elfie in her wake. A large brown LEFT LUGGAGE sign hung from the canopy over the final door, which was open to reveal a small room filled with stacked, old-fashioned suitcases, wicker baskets and leather trunks.

But no stationmaster.

'Ru,' Elfie whispered, trotting behind her. 'This isn't the Trowbridge you knew, is it? Can we please admit that now? If we accept the truth, then . . .'

'No,' Ru snapped. 'There's nothing strange. We're at Trowbridge. We just need to find someone who works here and then we go home. We could even charge our phones . . .' She glanced at the walls, but couldn't see any plug sockets. 'Or maybe we should just head out of the station and look for a taxi, or . . .'

She skidded to a halt.

Cribbins was striding confidently along the opposite platform, heading into the stationmaster's office.

Dread curdled in her throat.

'Did he see us?' Elfie gripped her arm.

'Don't think so.' She nodded to the Left Luggage room. 'In there.'

Ru pulled Elfie inside and gently pushed the door, wincing as it creaked shut. The room was plunged into darkness. She crept behind a tower of suitcases, huddling into Elfie, whose heartbeat was as fast as her own. She wished with everything she had that the cheery stationmaster found them before the Conductor did.

TWENTY-FIVE

The Left Luggage room stank powerfully of leather. Squashed inside a labyrinth of suitcases, Ru held her nose and tried not to gag.

Cribbins' footsteps were still far away enough to be on the opposite platform. But they wouldn't be for long.

At the far wall, a square window let in a latticed beam of pink light, and laser-like, it hit a pile of drab cases piled on a wheelbarrow. They were old, and adorned with straps and buckles, just like the ones on *The Green Lady*. There were no hard-shelled wheelie suitcases. No rucksacks, or sports bags or sparkles, or unicorns, or monster trucks or spots or flowers. All plain, plain, plain.

Elfie began to unclasp buckles and lift the lids.

'Oh my days,' she murmured.

'What is it?' Curiosity getting the better of her, Ru scrambled over. More vintage costumes were stuffed inside. Trousers and braces, stockings and skirts, lace-up shoes, glass potion bottles labelled *shampoo* and ceramic jars of face cream.

'Oh, look at this.' Elfie handed her a rectangular card, a painting of flowers on it. She flipped it over. It was a postcard – the address to somewhere in London, and a few lines of curly scrawls filled the other half.

> My dearest Paula,
> Bath is a dreadful bore. It is too quiet and brown, and I miss you and Dotty.
> There is a new Charlie Chaplin film playing at The Palace this weekend and I shall take you both, should Dotty do well at learning her sums and keeping out of trouble.
> All my love,
> Your Smithy.

'The stamp,' Elfie said quietly.

Ru reluctantly slid her eyes to the top corner of

the postcard. The stamp was red, with a face that was not King Charles III, but a younger man with an impossibly large moustache that flicked up at the ends. KING GEORGE V.

'Ru, why are you having trouble accepting this?' Elfie whispered. 'I thought you'd got it on the train, what with Malik and everything. We're stuck somewhere in time. A halfway place. I don't know. Nothing is the same.' Her tone was kind, and she spelt out the last few words like she was talking to a toddler.

Ru clenched her jaw, heat coursing through her cheeks and into her nostrils. 'It's just . . . the train was one thing. And Malik was . . .' Her voice cracked. 'I don't even know what Malik was. But on board, there was always the chance of escaping. Which we did, didn't we?' She looked up at Elfie and rubbed more tears away. 'But if this place . . . the outside world . . . is the same, then . . .' She swallowed. The thought was too big. 'Then how are we ever going to get back to our own time? How are we supposed to escape from here? Is this it? Are we trapped in the past now?'

A large part of her desperately hoped that Elfie

had the answer, but the other girl looked as lost as she was.

'Oh, Ru,' Elfie sighed and placed a warm arm around her shoulders. 'Bear hug coming up.'

Ru let herself relax into the cuddle, calming a bit at the comforting scent of cherries. 'I'm sorry I was wrong about the fields,' she mumbled. 'And that I've been so mean and snappy.'

'All forgiven.' Elfie smiled faintly. 'I really wish I had an answer for you, Ru. The only thing I *do* know is that sometimes, it's better to face the truth. Sometimes it's not possible for us to fix it. Sometimes, all we can do is embrace the unknown and hope we find a way through.'

'I think you're going to be a spiritual psychologist like your mum, Elfie.'

'No chance. I'm taking after my nana and playing the mandolin.'

They giggled under their breath, and Ru suddenly felt exhausted. She wanted to be in bed. She wanted Mum, with her made-up stories and her fluffy onesies and her silly, snorty laugh. She wanted Dad and his Cryptex hunts, his quiet thoughtfulness and the smell of his aftershave. She wanted them both.

Together or apart, it didn't matter any more. As long as they were with her.

The cheery stationmaster's voice rumbled through the walls. Impossible to make out where he was now. But the sound of him was a beacon of hope, wherever it came from.

'Do you think we can try just one more time?' Ru pleaded. 'Then that'll be it. Just in case there *is* a real, flesh-and-blood stationmaster. If I'm wrong, I'll step firmly out of denial and into the real world, or whatever world we're in right now, OK?'

Elfie took a deep breath. 'OK. I'm with you. What's the plan?'

Ru got to her feet. 'Right. The bell rings when you push open the café door. When we hear that, we'll know that Cribbins has gone in there. Then we can get out of here, run back to the stationmaster's office and wait for him to come back. I can hear him – he's got to be close by.'

Elfie grinned wryly. 'Nice and easy. So, we wait.'

They fell into a thick, charged silence. Ru wondered if Elfie could hear the loud throb of her pulse, the catch of breath in her throat.

After what seemed like hours, but was likely only

a minute or two, heavy strides descended the staircase. The executioner, approaching the gallows.

Thud, thud. Jangle jangle. Tick-tock.

Ru closed her eyes.

A door creaked open. A bell rang, and the door swung shut again, clicking back into place.

'He's in the café,' Ru hissed. 'Get out now!'

She threw the door open and ran faster than she ever had in her life, Elfie's feet pounding the platform behind her. She didn't even glimpse the café door as they passed, but tore up the stairs and across the walkway until breathing felt like knives stabbing her lungs.

They hurtled down the other steps, reached the stationmaster's office and threw themselves inside with the last thread of their strength.

Twenty-six

The stationmaster's office was empty still. They swiftly untangled themselves from the heap they'd landed in on the wooden floor, and Ru glanced out at the platform. Cribbins was blurred behind the frosted glass of the café window, but it looked like he was searching every nook and cranny; up and down, behind and under. Despite the chill of the night, Ru was sweating buckets. Between the running and the multiple layers and the adrenaline, she was practically liquid, and the fire crackling in the grate didn't help, either.

'Ru...' Elfie said gently.

But she already knew. She'd known the minute they'd fallen through the door. She didn't even have to look away from the café window. 'The Station

Master isn't coming, is he?'

'No. I don't think he is.'

Ru swallowed acid. 'Well, there we go.'

The stationmaster's desk was dark mahogany, with a homemade blanket thrown on the back of the wooden chair. Pens and small bottles of ink were lined up in an orderly fashion, with a closed leather book nearby. An enamel mug of something hot steamed on top of a pile of books, next to a tall telephone.

The fire hissed, and a spark of orange flew on to the rug. Ru stamped on it furiously, even after it had faded to black.

'Are you all right?' Elfie asked.

'I . . . I . . .' An idea struck Ru, and she stopped stamping. One more chance. 'Just let me try calling someone. I'll be quick.'

Elfie nodded solemnly. 'Do you know how to?'

'I didn't spend every weekend of Year 2 watching *Mary Poppins* on repeat and not learn how to use a vintage phone, Elfie.' Ru darted to the desk and lifted the receiver.

Elfie's smile looked a little sad.

Ru jiggled a lever knowledgeably. 'I think that

gets the attention of the operator – oh yes, hello?'

Her heart leapt as a fuzzy, clipped voice rang out from the telephone. 'Number please?'

This was it. Ru gripped the phone until her fingers hurt. 'Emergency services, please. 999.'

'Number, please?'

'I . . . I just said, sorry, 999. Police, fire officers, whatever.'

'Number, please? Is anyone there?'

No. Ru looked up at Elfie, hope dying.

They can't hear you, she mouthed.

'999?' Desperate, Ru tried again. It came out as a small squeak.

There was a *click* from the other end of the phone, and silence.

The last of her hope vanished with the operator. That was it. There was nothing left to try.

'So now we know. You were right.' She shivered, her sweat running cold as ice.

'I'm sorry,' Elfie said. 'I didn't want to be.'

Ru wasn't sure she had any energy left for talking. Instead, she let her eyes wander helplessly around the room. It was cluttered and comfortable, and probably welcoming in any other situation. Cast-iron train lamps were stacked in a row, alongside portraits of railway employees. Shelves were bursting with hardback books, and pinned to the walls were timetables for train lines that didn't exist any more.

Except they do exist, don't they? Ru shuddered.

Strangest of all, a clock hung above the desk with hands frozen at 5.05. The pendulum was pointing diagonally to the left, like it had been glued there mid-swing.

But it wasn't the clock that made Ru stop in her tracks.

'Wait. Hang on. Elfie, look at the photograph on the wall.'

Men lined up in old MWL uniforms in front of a giant train. It was the same as the smashed portrait from Gram's gallery wall, only this one was mould-free. Ru stared at it until her eyes watered.

Even drained of colour, the train was strikingly familiar. She knew what the caption was going to say before she looked.

April 1925. Crew of The Green Lady.

All her fight ebbed away. She couldn't deny it any more. She'd known which train she was on, hadn't she? She'd known for a long time.

The gold bow shoes, the tin of Rolled Ox Tongue. The stationmaster's call. '*. . . all wearing antlers and paint . . . up at the Tor, later!*' The May Day song from the next carriage, eternally stuck on the same verse. Station Ned. Malik. The headlines in the museum.

DAWN GLASTONBURY VIADUCT DERAILMENT. ONLY DRIVER AND STOKER SURVIVE

MELBRIDGE TRAGEDY: TRAIN CRASH KILLS ALMOST ENTIRE HAMLET

SEMAPHORE SIGNAL MISSED? QUESTIONS RAISED OVER DRIVER'S RESPONSIBILITY

The Conductor's uniform and the skeleton cat in the display case; the pocket watch, frozen at 5.05.

The clock's pendulum. 5.05. *The Green Lady's* numberplate. 0505.

That was the time of the crash, wasn't it?

Great-Great-Grampy Syd stood in his place at the back of the photograph, still turned slightly away from the man next to him. And this time, Ru knew the man's face. Unsmiling, half-masked by his moustache, with piercing eyes that bore through the ink and glass. There was no mistaking him; not for a second. It was Cribbins.

Everything suddenly made sickening sense.

'At 5.05 a.m. on the morning of the first of May, 1925 . . .' Ru said, numbly, '*The Green Lady* was transporting MWL staff to the Green Man Festival at Glastonbury Tor. It derailed on Glastonbury Viaduct. All but two were killed.'

'Oh my days.' Elfie appeared at her shoulder with a sharp intake of breath. 'The man in the middle.' She touched the face of a young, serious-looking man in overalls. He was clean-shaven, with a strong jaw and a cleft chin, like Elfie. 'He looks just like my dad. That's unbelievable. And . . . oh. Ru.' Her tone changed. 'Look in the background.'

Ru dropped her gaze to a small shape beside the train, and her breath caught in her throat. It was blurry, but it was clearly a boy in a waistcoat and linen trousers with a two-tone cat draped over his shoulders.

'Oh, Malik,' she murmured. 'I'm so sorry.'

Thud, thud. Jangle jangle. Tick-tock.

'Listen!' Elfie grabbed her. 'Cribbins is on the walkway. He'll be down these stairs any second!'

Terror hit Ru like a bolt of lightning. 'Elfie, listen. We get outside the station now – head to the fields. You were right, it's our only chance. Get low and keep to the shadows. Go, go, go!'

She raced out of the office and on to the platform, Elfie hot on her heels. The walkway thundered above them with Cribbins' threatening tread, getting nearer to the staircase with each second.

But they'd make it out of the station before that. They'd *have* to.

The exit was in touching distance. Ru kept the old factory building locked in her eyeline, and found herself in a vast, empty courtyard of sandy-coloured grit. The factory was open and alive, spreading the smell of pork pies across the town.

No flats. They hadn't converted it yet.

Her world had well and truly gone.

'Look, there's a shop opposite.' Ru was hoarse. 'Over there.'

They ran inside the grocery store, where trays of fruit and vegetables were laid out beneath a striped awning, and hid themselves underneath the counter. Stacks of the day's unopened newspapers were tied with brown string.

The headlines shouted in black-and-white typewriter print.

WILTSHIRE TIMES

KING GEORGE V ON RECUPERATIVE CRUISE

**STRONG WINDS RAVAGE
THE WEST COUNTRY**

ESCAPED GOAT IN LIMPLEY STOKE

**MWL STAFF EMBARK ON
ANNUAL GLASTONBURY TRIP**

1 MAY 1925

Overcome, Ru put her head between her legs before she could pass out. There was no escaping it. They were stuck in the past, with no way home.

TWENTY-SEVEN

Thud, thud. Jangle jangle. Tick-tock.

He was getting nearer with every passing second. The tread of heavy shoes on grit. The rapidly encroaching chill. Elfie linked her fingers in Ru's as they crouched under the counter.

'It's OK,' she soothed, sounding more scared than Ru. 'It's OK.'

'Look at the newspaper. This is what it's all about, Elfie.'

Elfie's brows knitted. 'The escaped goat?'

There was a beat, and the two of them broke into hysterical laughter.

'Sssh! N . . . not the goat, you idiot . . .' Tears streamed from Ru's eyes, and she didn't know if it was the goat, or the fear, or both. 'You were right about Glastonbury.'

Elfie was holding her ribs in an attempt to calm down. 'The f-final stop?'

'Yeah,' Ru replied, laughter fading. Suddenly it didn't seem so funny. 'There was an accident on Glastonbury Viaduct. Everyone died, except for my grampy and one other person. For some reason Cribbins is making it all happen again and I'm so sorry for doubting you, Elfie; you were right about all of it and I should have listened.'

Elfie sighed, and it was heavy with unsaid things. 'Don't be sorry. I wish I *was* wrong. But I don't get why. Why would he relive his own horrible death and bring us along for the ride? Why make Malik relive it? What's wrong with him?'

'I wish I knew.'

They stared at the small photograph of the train in the bottom corner of the newspaper. It was being cleaned and polished by railway workers, Malik among them. He was beaming proudly. A cloth was scrunched in his hand, and Station Ned was splayed at his feet, paws up.

'Look how happy he is.' Ru shuffled even closer to Elfie. 'It's not fair.'

'No,' Elfie said quietly. 'His whole life just *stolen* from him. Who knows what he would've . . .' She clamped her hand over her mouth. Eyes wide in horror, she pointed up.

The door swung open with a painful creak.

Tick-tock.

Familiar footsteps thudded across the stone floor to the other side of the counter, carrying the stench of mildew and mould. Goosebumps rose on Ru's neck as she felt the white heat of anger burn from him.

Tick-tock.

Her head was about to burst, but she couldn't take her eyes off the newspaper and Malik's unknowing smile. Right now, she was more terrified than she'd ever been. So how on earth had Malik felt, knowing he was falling to his death? How had the girl with the doll felt? How had Syd lived with the knowledge of what had happened?

'Tick-tock.' Cribbins' call was barely a whisper.

Dragon breaths, Ru.

Just like Mum had taught her, she took a deep inhale from the pit of her stomach and imagined breathing out plumes of fire.

Her brain fell quiet, and with an ice-cold certainty, Ru knew what she was going to do. Oddly calm, she touched Elfie's hand. *I'm sorry*, she mouthed. *Stay down.*

What? Elfie mouthed in alarm. *What are you doing?*

With one final inhale, Ru forced her trembling legs to stand.

'Ru, *no!*'

Tick-tock.

The Conductor's back was to her, a thin shadow in the moonlight. He turned in a juddering circle, and Ru's legs buckled. She clutched the counter to stop herself collapsing, because his eyelids had gone. His blue eyes bulged from their sockets, and his mouth broke into its wide, strange smile.

Ru wanted to run far, far away from the zombie nightmare in shredded clothes. He was barely human now. More the living dead. But she wasn't going to run any more.

'Miss Cole,' he purred, all velvet. 'And Miss Midwinter?'

'I'm Miss Darke, not Miss Cole. And Elfie's not with...'

A shout cut her off.

'Here!' Elfie jumped up like a jack-in-the-box. 'You're not getting rid of me that easily.'

Thank you, Ru mouthed. She was glad she wasn't alone.

Cribbins tipped his hat, and tufts of brown hair spiralled to the ground. 'I regret to say that you both alighted at the wrong stop. But there's no need to worry. We'll soon be back on track and on to our final destination.'

TWENTY-EIGHT

Her chest hollow, Ru trailed with Elfie behind the Conductor.

'You did it for him, didn't you?' Elfie whispered at her side. 'Malik.'

Ru nodded, tightening her hands into fists. 'Malik.'

Every footstep felt like walking over hot coals. But Ru wasn't going to let him die alone. Not this time.

She just wished she knew what to do.

'Have you got a plan?'

'Not yet. I'll think of something.'

'No, Ru,' Elfie said firmly. '*We'll* think of something.'

The Green Lady was a monster waiting up ahead; a dormant dragon with smoke pouring from its nostrils. Flickering shadows of the ghostly passengers moved across the window, their music tinny and voices faint.

Winter time has gone and past-o.

Oh, shut up, Ru thought.

Steam burst from the chimney as Cribbins ushered them up the steps and on to the train. It surrounded her and caught in her throat, and made her ears stuffy as cotton wool.

When the door of Coach C opened, the stale stench almost made her turn around and run into the night. She'd thought she'd left it for ever. But there Malik was, his jaw slack with shock, looking heartbroken, and she remembered why she'd returned.

'Oh, no,' he moaned.

'As you can see' – Cribbins rubbed his peeling hands together – 'I've prepared a feast to celebrate your return. Your misadventure must have made you hungry, but fear not; Coach C has everything you could possibly need. There will be no need to leave again. Not until the final stop.'

Plates of hot food towered on the tables: roast potatoes and beef, gravy and vegetables.

Just when I thought it couldn't get any worse.

'I will leave you to settle back in. Time is of the essence, and we are behind.'

In the blink of an eye, Cribbins was gone, and Ru forced herself not to cry as the key turned in the lock.

Trapped again.

The broken window was fixed, with no sign that it had been smashed to smithereens barely an hour ago.

I hate you glowed scarlet in the corner, mocking them.

Station Ned snored gently on Malik's lap. The purple bruise on the boy's face had spread down to his neck, and his ripped waistcoat was crusty with dirt.

'That must hurt,' Elfie said.

'Not any more,' he replied.

The whistle screamed and the train roared to life. Back and forth they swayed, like rag dolls, and the Victorian factory buildings of Trowbridge thinned into crimson-tinted countryside.

'I'm sorry for making you leave, Elfie,' Ru said. 'And for making you come back, too.'

'Pah.' Elfie blew a raspberry and climbed cross-legged on to an armchair. 'We tried. That's better than not trying. He was always going to find us, Ru. At least we got to decide how.'

'Mmm.'

'He didn't catch you?' Malik said. 'Why did you come back?'

'What can I say? We missed the food.' Ru gave a wry grin and lowered herself into an armchair.

Malik smiled sadly, and Ru took him in with new eyes. He still looked younger than her and Elfie. But she saw something else now, too, lurking beneath. The accident had left scars, inside and out.

'I'm so sorry we abandoned you, Malik,' she said.

'Don't be. I wish you'd stayed away.'

'Rude.'

He smiled for real at that. 'So how much do you know?'

'A lot.' Ru peeled off the extra layers of clothing until it felt like she could breathe again. 'How long have we got until Glastonbury?'

'About forty minutes.'

'Oh.' A pang in Ru's stomach bent her double, and she clutched the back of her chair for strength. *Forty minutes to figure something out. Or we're dead.*

'What do you remember, Malik?' she asked

carefully, wary of pushing too hard. 'When did you figure it all out? If . . . if that's OK to ask. There's not exactly a manual for this.'

Malik looked suddenly worried. 'I would've told you if I remembered about it from the beginning, I *swear*. I would never have let you get on.'

'We know,' Elfie and Ru chorused.

'It was like . . .' He stroked Ned softly, and the cat's purr rumbled like the wheels of a train. 'It was like waking up from a fever. Groggy, not sure where I was, just like I'd been asleep. At first, I thought nothing was different. I mean, why would I?'

Snippets of conversation came back to Ru. The lie about his ticket.

I . . . I will find it. I promise. I think perhaps my mother has it? She's . . . she's in the other coach. Perhaps . . . perhaps I can go and get it from her?

'With each stop we passed, more things came back to me, even if they were all muddled. When you two got on I panicked, especially when you started talking about things I didn't understand, like phones and signal – really, how are those little metal boxes telephones? – and cameras with screens and batteries and wearing trousers and multicoloured hair and teeth braces that don't shred your mouth.'

Elfie shrugged. 'Sometimes they do.'

'Then after one station, my waistcoat was suddenly torn. And after another, this happened.' He gestured to the bruise. 'When Ned escaped, I remembered everything. That is, almost everything.' He scratched the cat underneath his chin, and Ned purred even louder. 'I just needed my best friend.'

Like she did with Grizabella, Ru held out a hand and made a kissing sound through her teeth. The cat's nose twitched, and he edged forward in cautious pads.

'I found him when he was a kitten,' Malik said fondly. 'Little fool had got himself stuck in a pipe. Since then, we've gone everywhere together, even when we're not supposed to.'

'Like this train?' Elfie asked.

'Like this train. Stupid thing is, neither of us were supposed to be on board. Did you know that?'

'No,' Ru said. 'What do you mean?'

'My father had an accident in the boiler shop, so we couldn't go on the trip. I just... just wanted to see them off, that was all. It was so windy that day. Ned got scared and ran on to the train, so I followed him.

He refused to come out of the cabinet and I didn't want to leave him, so I lied about my ticket, and before we knew it, the train had left. I wish I'd stayed where I was.'

He didn't have to say the rest. *Then I'd never have died.*

Ru was itching to ask more, but she didn't want to push him to the point of no return. 'Last question Malik, I promise. You said you remembered almost everything. What's missing?'

'I . . .' He began shaking so violently, Ned's fur blurred.

'Ru . . .' Elfie warned.

'The final few moments,' Malik whispered. 'The . . . the big moment. I know it happened. But it's just a blank. I'm sorry.'

'Don't you dare apologize, Malik Marley.'

Elfie put her hand on Ru's shoulder, and reassuring warmth seeped through her jumper. Elfie knew what she was thinking, didn't she?

How are we going to stop it if we don't know what happened?

She let her outstretched hand drop. Station Ned watched it fall, then balanced on the edge of Malik's lap with an annoyed mew.

Just like Grizabella. Ru made the kissing sound again. The cat leapt into the air towards her, a two-tone blur of black and grey that promptly floated through her legs. He landed on the seat cushion beneath her, looking perplexed.

'Whoa!' Ru exclaimed. The cat huffed, then turned into a circle and settled on the chair, his tiny triangular ears poking out of her thigh. 'What is *happening*?'

'You can't feel him at all?' Malik asked incredulously. 'He's a lump.'

'No! It's just like warm water. Seriously, it's *so* weird.'

'That fits. Look at these.' Nose to camera screen, Elfie scampered to her side. She scrolled through pictures of the eclipse, and the dark shape of *The Green Lady*, until she landed on a shot of an empty chair and two patches of misty fog hovering above the table.

'This was when Cribbins was asking about Malik's ticket.' She tapped the screen. 'They were definitely both there when I took the picture.'

She scrolled through other snaps of the refreshment trolley, the suitcases, the oil lamps glinting, the armchair and tables. Occasionally Ru appeared, big-haired and anxious-faced, but wherever Malik or the Conductor had been, there were only the patches of fog.

'So we know I'm definitely dead,' Malik said drily.

'Well, that's kind of the reason we came back, Malik,' Ru volunteered finally. 'We need to figure out...'

Winter time has gone and past-o,
Summer time has come at last-o.

Ru's blood turned cold. What had once sounded like celebration now felt eerily like the chanting of a curse.

TWENTY-NINE

Another station emerged from the darkness: a simple, one-platformed hut that floated across the window and out of sight. The night was too smoke-filled to see the sign, to identify where they were, but it didn't really matter, anyway.

The music played on. Steam poured past the windows as the train began to slow, and the whistle hailed the upcoming station with its cry.

'Any second now,' Ru said grimly.

On cue, the threatening thud of Cribbins' shoes sounded from the corridor. Then came the keys' metallic *clink* and his watch's insistent *tick-tock*. Counting down to their death.

Station Ned's hairs pricked up in a single line down his back. He hissed and jumped back into

Malik's waiting arms.

'Here we go again.' Ru braced herself. What would they face this time? A walking skeleton? A fiery demon from hell?

Elfie sprang up as if she'd been tasered.

'The food!' she cried. 'We haven't eaten the food!'

Ru glared at the steaming plates of stodge. She'd never felt less like eating. 'Ugh, if he thinks force-feeding us will keep us here, he's more deranged than I thought.'

'He's trying to entice us,' Elfie said. 'So we won't want to leave. To be honest I think he's been dead so long he's forgotten what an enjoyable amount of food looks like.'

'About fifteen courses fewer, that's what.'

Ru scooped up the plates, clambered on to the armchair, opened a luggage cabinet and tipped the food inside. Gravy dripped from the ledge and on to her hair.

The key turned in the lock. Heart thudding, she slammed the cabinet door, wiped the brown mess away and began to alight, but her foot caught in the gap between chair back and seat and she hurtled downwards. She could only watch, horrified, as the plates flew out of her hands and fell to the ground with a *smash*. Shards of white china spread across the floor, pocked by dark splodges of gravy.

'Elfie, help!' They gathered up the pieces hurriedly, slicing their skin and drawing blood.

Another oil lamp shattered, as if hit by a bullet.

Tick-tock.

Ru and Elfie froze.

Cribbins stood at the doorway, blanketed in shadow. 'Had an accident, Miss Cole?'

Stupefied, Ru looked down at the plates. 'I . . . I slipped.'

'What a surprise. I presume you finished your supper?'

'Oh, yes!' Elfie interjected shrilly. 'The best course yet. It was delicious, thank you.'

'My pleasure.' Cribbins smiled humbly and lifted his hat. What little remained of his hair was matted with blood that oozed from the diagonal slash across his head. The last of his unmarked skin stretched thinly across his cheekbones, the strange fish-hook smile pasted across his face. 'I am here to serve you,' he said. 'There is still more food to come, of course.'

The colour drained from Elfie's face. 'Oh, goody,'

she said meekly.

The train juddered. Station Ned rolled off Malik's lap and hit the table, yowling in protest. Whip-fast, Cribbins snapped round with a sneer. 'What is *that*?' he snarled.

Malik shrank into the window, pulling the feline back to him. 'He's not doing any harm, Mr Cribbins, I'll look after him . . .'

In the blink of an eye, the Conductor shot out his arm and grabbed Ned by the scruff of his neck. The cat hissed and spat, legs dangling uselessly. Cribbins bared his teeth and hissed back, and Ned fell still, his fur standing on end.

'Cats do not belong on trains, Malik Marley.'

'Please, sir, let me . . .' Malik began, but before he could utter another word, Cribbins marched out of the carriage, locking the door behind him, and in a heartbeat boy and cat were torn apart.

'Malik.' Elfie's arms twitched, like she wanted to hug him. 'Are you OK?'

He didn't answer. A patch of red appeared on his hand, and Ru watched in horrid fascination as a wound bloomed from thumb to middle finger. But Malik didn't flinch. A glaze had settled over his face, as if he were somewhere else entirely.

'That's what he said then.' He sounded far away. 'No cats on the train.'

Wait. He remembers?

Despite everything, she felt something dormant bubble in the pit of her stomach.

Feverish with excitement, Ru swerved to face Elfie. Her friend raised a cryptic eyebrow. *Tread lightly*.

'Then what happened, Malik?' Ru pressed, as gently as she could. 'Do you remember?'

Elfie stretched out her arm to comfort him, but Malik moved away. 'Every other conductor let Station Ned on. Everyone except Mr Cribbins. We almost got away with it, but just as the journey was about to end he snatched Ned, and then the train just started . . .' He scrunched up his face. 'It sort of started screaming.'

'Screaming?'

'I don't know. There was just this almighty noise – I'd never heard the like – and then I was flying, and so was Ned, and at least I managed to catch him so we were holding each other . . . and Mr Cribbins had the most awful look on his face. I think it was shock. And then . . . then I woke up here.' He rubbed his eyes. 'Nobody deserves that fate.'

The lunar eclipse filled most of the windows with red light now, as if the moon had doubled in size. Everything beyond that was blurred with smoke.

'Malik, shall I tell you what the screaming and flying was?' Ru asked softly. 'I don't have to if it's too hard.'

He thought for a moment. Ru could see the fight raging in him. 'Yes please,' he said finally. 'I think I need to know.'

Ru took a breath. Malik's bruised face was an open book, and finding the right words was harder than she'd expected. Randomly, she thought of Mum and Dad, and how they would have felt breaking the news of their split to her and Sam. They must have been *terrified*.

'The train derailed on Glastonbury Viaduct,' she said at last. 'And only two people survived, the driver and the stoker. It ruined Melbridge. I'm so sorry, Malik.'

Ru sat back, respectfully gifting him the space to let it sink in. But to her surprise, Malik didn't look heartbroken, or even wistful. His brow was furrowed in confusion.

'But, wait,' he frowned. 'If only the driver and the stoker survived, that would mean that the cab made it across the viaduct and the passenger coaches didn't. That doesn't make any logical sense. How would that happen? Unless...'

'Unless what?' Ru's heart thumped.

'Unless the coupling was damaged. But they always check everything like that before departing.'

'Well,' Ru admitted reluctantly, 'there was talk of the driver being to blame...'

'No,' said Malik, with a decided firmness that Ru had never seen. 'Absolutely not. Syd Cole was the driver that day, and I'd trust him with my life. There is *no* way he was to blame.'

THIRTY

The train sped on relentlessly through the patchwork quilt of brambles and fields. Scarlet beams flooded the windows. Ru felt like a long-broken light had been fixed.

'Malik, Syd Cole spent the rest of his days convinced he was to blame for the accident. It wrecked his whole life.'

'No. He wasn't just a good man, or a good driver,' Malik explained. 'He was the best of both. What he didn't know about trains wasn't worth knowing.'

Ru smiled. 'I've heard that before.'

'He was teaching me everything he knew. *"We'll make a driver out of you yet, Malik Marley,"* that's what he used to say; and I wasn't supposed to amount to anything except cleaning in the Engine

Shed. Then he became the youngest MWL driver ever, and he was so proud, and *so* prepared. I promise, there's no chance it was his fault.'

Elfie nudged Ru softly. 'Tell him. Tell him who you are.'

'Who you are?' Malik asked. 'What do you mean?'

'Malik...' Ru said, 'Syd was my great-great-grandfather.'

'Syd Cole?' Malik gaped at her. 'You're related to Sydney Cole?' He scrutinized her, then burst into surprised chuckles. 'Of course you are! You've got his hair! That and the falling over. That man had more bruises than I do.'

Ru rolled her eyes. 'Yeah, thanks for that, Syd. Clumsiness and giant hair – a great inheritance.' She hesitated. 'He never drove a train again.'

Malik's face fell, and even as she said it, Ru wondered if she should have kept her mouth shut. But there was no time left for secrets. Literally.

'That would've pleased Cribbins at least, had he lived,' Malik said bitterly. 'He hated Syd.'

'What?' Something clicked, like magnets connecting. 'Cribbins hated Syd Cole?'

'*Really* hated him.' Malik frowned. 'Jim Cribbins was always quiet. He was a stickler for order, and was grumpy sometimes – especially with Ned – but he wasn't unkind, really, except to Syd. Mind you, Syd gave as good as he got. You could hear them yelling at each other across the platforms most days.'

'Why did they hate each other?'

'They grew up together. Even born on the same day. Dad said they'd been childhood best friends, but what with competing for glory and that sort of thing, the friendship turned into rivalry. Syd thought Jim Cribbins was a finickity goody-two-shoes. Cribbins thought Syd was a lazy, irresponsible show-off. Then Syd became the driver, and Cribbins was livid. He was hurt, really, even I could see that, but it came out as nastiness. Said he didn't trust Syd as far as he could throw him.'

Sparks flew across Ru's synapses.

I hate you, marked indelibly on the window.

The two men in the portrait, facing away from each other.

You arrogant swine . . . Have you forgotten how you failed everybody . . . you're nothing but a reckless, swaggering failure . . . follow me *for once . . .*

'So . . .' Ru's thoughts were as fragile as glass. 'Cribbins already had it in for Syd, especially when he became this superstar driver. Then Syd drove the staff on their trip – the trip in which nearly all the passengers died, Cribbins included. Syd blamed himself and spent the rest of his life under suspicion.'

'What are you saying?' Elfie looked doubtful. 'That Cribbins somehow staged the whole thing to destroy Syd?'

'I don't think he'd go *that* far,' Malik said. 'Given that he ended up dead.'

Ru shook her head. 'I'm saying that Cribbins – already convinced that Syd's a total loser – died on that very train journey, and he thinks Syd messed up, doesn't he? He died thinking Syd's responsible, and he's angry.'

'Why do all of this, though?' Elfie twisted her mermaid hair into frayed, overwrought tangles. 'Syd's already dead – sorry, Malik – so what's the point?'

Exhausted, Ru collapsed into the chair's cushion. 'Yep, Syd's well dead. But I'm not though, am I? And neither are you, Elfie.'

'*Me?* What have I got to do with anything?'

Ru turned to Malik. 'One more question for you. Do you remember the stoker's name? He was the only other survivor.'

Malik narrowed his eyes. 'Yes, I do!' His face softened into a smile. 'It was Henry. Always had a smile and a song, he did. Henry Midwinter.'

Elfie gasped. 'That's *my* name! The . . . picture in the office . . . the one that looked like my dad.'

And there it was. The final connecting thread. Ru was surprised by how little it surprised her.

'So, we're both related to the survivors.' Elfie's look was charged with electricity, and a current buzzed between them. 'I don't think that's a coincidence, is it?'

'No. I don't think it is. This whole thing is a massive revenge plot. And he's making Malik relive it, because . . .'

'Because he blames me, too,' Malik said quietly. 'Cribbins died in Coach C because of me and Ned.' His cheeks sank into hollows as he stared at a spot across the aisle. The chair beside the *I hate you* graffiti. 'He'd spent most of the journey in the cab, because he didn't trust Syd. That's what he said. He wanted to keep an eye on him and make sure he was driving properly.'

'Bet Syd loved that,' said Ru.

Malik didn't take his eyes from the chair. 'We weren't far from Glastonbury. On his final walk-around, Cribbins caught Ned climbing out of the cabinet. *"No damn cat's going to be let loose in the first-class dining carriage, Malik Marley,"* he said. *"Don't move from your seat. I'm keeping watch until we arrive in Glastonbury, and then I'm telephoning your father and putting you on another train home."'* Malik nodded to the empty chair. 'And he sat there in a mood until we ... until it happened. *Don't move from your seat*, he said. And I haven't, have I? Not for a moment.'

'So there we have it,' Elfie whispered. 'A blood moon, a ley line, May Eve and the ancestors of your sworn enemies. All the ingredients for a giant revenge cake.'

THIRTY-ONE

Darkness swallowed the windows as they entered another tunnel. This one was longer than the others; all Ru could make out was an endless reel of bricks and black, spots of lamp-glow and four terrified eyes. Finally, the train emerged, headfirst into a brute wind that shook and rattled the windows with a howl. There was a shock of silver light, and a clear, round moon.

'But . . .' She sat upright, instantly alert. 'Where's the eclipse gone?'

'Oh no,' Elfie whispered.

The look on Malik's face made her stomach turn over. He was gazing out at the miniature landscape of a city, stony and sombre in the distance.

'I remember this.' His voice cracked in fear. 'I

remember this.'

Through the thick haze of fog, a tiny pinprick of a shape began to form far across the fields. A rounded lump of a hill. Perched on top was a single tower pointing to the sky.

Glastonbury.

'What?' Ru climbed on the chair in alarm. 'We can't be there already, surely? It's too soon!'

'Oh my days,' came Elfie's husky whisper through the twilight. 'Look.'

A thin green bud grew from a crack above the doorway, juddering and writhing like it was on time lapse. As they watched, it formed into the shape of a long hanging garland, blooming with leaves and vines, entwined with coloured ribbons. Blue, red, purple, green. On the coach ceiling, more garlands grew, dozens draping across from one side of the ceiling to another.

Winter time has gone and past-o
Summer time has come at last-o

'But we haven't figured it out!' Ru cried. 'We don't know how to stop the accident yet!'

A warm hand slipped into hers. A waft of sweet cherries. 'Ru...'

We shall sing and dance the day...
Come followin' the Green Man that brings the May

Ru's head swam with fear. 'No, Elfie, listen,' she pleaded. 'Please. This isn't like Trowbridge. I want to try and make this right. *Please.*'
'But how? Ru, there's no time left.'

So, Hail! Hail! The First of May-o!
For it is the first summer's day-o!
Cast your cares and fears away,
Drink to the Green Man on the First of May!

'This is as it was.' Malik curled up on himself. 'Everything.'
The shape of a swift dived through the smoke and flew alongside the train. It fought against the wind with all its strength, slicing the air with its forked tail.
At that moment, Ru wished she could fly more than anything; she longed for the freedom she'd tasted when she'd leapt out of the train, to be caught

and cradled by the fresh air and carried by the wind. But fresh air and freedom seemed so far out of reach now.

The swift curved away from the window, gliding towards the semaphore signal that appeared on the horizon. It glowed ominously in the moon's rays. *CAUTION*. The horizontal signal arm wobbled precariously in the gale, and even from far away, Ru could see it losing its battle to stay in place.

Stay in place. It hit her like a bolt of lightning.

What had that headline said in the museum?

SEMAPHORE SIGNAL MISSED? QUESTIONS RAISED OVER DRIVER'S RESPONSIBILITY

'Ru, you've got that look on your face.' Elfie tugged at her hand. 'What is it?'

It was so windy that day. Ned got scared and ran on to the train.

'Ru?'

I must apologize for the slight bump we experienced near Silbury Hill earlier. The wind is picking up, and fallen leaves rendered the tracks slippery.

Ru stared at the trees that encircled the base of

Glastonbury Tor. Their leaves were ripped from their branches and snatched by the wind, and they wound their way towards the train tracks like a flock of birds.

'I think . . .' Her words were slowed by terror. 'I know what happened . . .'

'In the accident?' Elfie searched her face keenly. 'What? Can we stop it?'

'Stop it?' Malik suddenly looked wildly hopeful. 'You can stop it?'

'I . . . I don't know. Newspapers thought Syd missed the caution signal, so didn't slow and went up the viaduct too fast. But what if he didn't miss it? What if the wind knocked it? If the signal arm was in the wrong place, then Syd would have thought it was safe to keep going at that speed even when it wasn't . . .'

'If the semaphore had worked, the train would've slowed?' Malik climbed up on the seat to kneeling, his fingers digging into the velvet. 'And we'd never . . .' His face crumpled. 'But wait, even if that were the case, that doesn't explain the back carriages derailing. That could easily happen anywhere.'

'I know.' Ru forced the speeding thunder of her

heart to slow. 'Listen. The Conductor said himself – the bump at Silbury Hill was caused by leaves falling on to the track. What if it happened again, near Glastonbury? The wind blew the leaves on the track, the train slipped, and the coupling was damaged. Nobody would've known. And it wouldn't have been an issue if the semaphore signal was in the right place. Syd would've gone slower up the viaduct and wouldn't have had to brake so suddenly, so high up. Do you remember a bump before the crash, Malik? Is it even possible that's what happened?'

'Yes,' he said, wearing an unfamiliar expression. It resembled hope. 'Yes, that's exactly what happened. It's not just possible, Ru. It's the answer.' He took a long, lifeless breath that filled his hollow chest. 'I want to go and warn Syd...'

Ru's stomach leapt.

'But...' He turned green. Ru hadn't known that ghosts could turn green. 'I can't get up from this chair, can I? He told me I can't get up from this chair.'

'Oh, Malik...' Ru whispered, hit with a pang of affection for him. His darting anxiety. His bravery. He was torn in two.

She knelt at his feet, as close as she dared. He didn't move away.

'Losing control is horrible, isn't it?' Ru said. 'It's like... you're at the mercy of other people, and most other people make really *stupid* decisions. There's no safety in it. Like... you're climbing a tree and you're trying to find a branch to stand on, but there's none there and you just know you're going to fall. Is that how you feel, Malik? With the chair, and Station Ned and everything?'

He bobbed his head, not looking at her.

'This is new to me,' Ru grinned bashfully. 'But I guess there are some things we can't control, and we have to let those go even if it really hurts. But there are other times when we can fight like crazy to make things right. This is *your* time, Malik.'

He swallowed and glanced at Ru. 'I'm going to leave my chair,' he said, and with all the strength and dignity of a soldier marching over the top, he got to his feet.

Ru swelled with pride. 'Malik Marley, you might be the bravest person I've ever met.'

He offered her a crooked smile. 'I feel so strange.'

A flash of green from the window, and the *GO* light

of the semaphore signal glowed through like an orb.

But it shouldn't be green! Ru wanted to yell. *Caution! Slow down!*

But of course, nothing changed, and the train didn't slow. Instead, it sped faster towards the viaduct, and *The Green Lady*'s whistle blew out its swansong.

'The whistle's gone,' Elfie croaked. 'He's coming.'

Pop, pop, pop.

All of the remaining lights in the carriage went out, one after another, and exploded into showers of glass.

THIRTY-TWO

'Get down!' Ru cried, yanking Elfie to the floor. They covered their heads and ducked under the seat. The pale, ghostly light made it too dark to see far, so Ru fumbled for Dad's headtorch and switched it on with trembling fingers.

The last lamp shattered, and the haunting tune drifted through the wood. It didn't seem at all merry any more. It put Ru in mind of hooded figures from horror stories: heads bowed, offerings made. Demons summoned from the darkness.

Blue bells they have started to ring-o . . .

Bluebells?
Ru swung the headtorch to one of Cribbins'

precious vases, catching the violet flower in its beam. Delicate petals sparkled with water droplets.

And true love, it is the thing-o . . .

Why was Cribbins so obsessed with the vases? Why had the exact same flowers decorated Trowbridge station? What was so special about them?

Love on any other day
Is never quite the same as on the First of May

'For all their bombast, those from the Otherworld are at the mercy of common garden plants.' That's what Gram had said. *'Flowers can summon them and they can banish them.'*

What if . . . ?

'Elfie, listen . . .' Ru said breathlessly. 'The flowers Cribbins doesn't want us to touch. What's the cream blossom called?'

Elfie raised her head to look. 'Hawthorn. Why?'

Ru's heart galloped. 'Gram told me that plants can have powers. She gave us yellow flowers as protection. Cribbins is so territorial about those vases – maybe . . . ?'

'Oh!' Elfie's nails dug into Ru's arm. 'You beautiful

genius, you! Bluebells and hawthorns are traditionally gathered around May Day, cos they're said to summon those from the other side, and to give them a safe haven ...'

'Spirits, demons and tricksters ... ?' Ru finished. 'Like Cribbins?'

'Exactly! So maybe if they were all gone, then ...'

'Maybe it would stop him, and Malik could go and warn Syd?'

'*Exactly.*'

A final, dying refrain and the song ended with an eruption of cheers. Or perhaps it was screams. It was impossible to tell any more.

'Time, Ru . . .' Elfie said nervously. 'The song never got this far before.'

The pressure built in Ru's temples and threatened to explode out of her ears like steam.

Tick-tock. Tick-tock.

Did that come from her own fevered mind? Or from something else?

'Quick, Elfie! The vases!' Ru's headtorch beam pointing the way, they ran down the length of the carriage and emptied all of the vases on to the floor. Blossoms and water splashed and tumbled on to their feet.

There was a moan from Malik's chair. Ru turned the torch to see him panting, pressed against the window.

'Are you OK?' Ru called, suddenly petrified. 'Do we need to stop?'

'N . . . no,' came the answer. 'Destroy them when I've gone to Syd.'

Thud. Jangle. Tick-tock.

'Everyone over here!' Ru hissed. 'The minute he opens that door, you two run to the cab.'

'But what about you?' Elfie demanded. 'We're not leaving you with him, and it's not like I can help with Syd anyway . . .'

Tick-tock. Multiple keys jangled. The sound of the executioner at dawn.

'I'll be right behind you. I'll destroy the flowers, make sure Cribbins is locked away and then I'll run.' Ru leant into Elfie's ear. 'Malik needs you,' she whispered. 'Even if you can't do anything, he needs to know you're there. Be strong for him.'

Eyes cast down, Elfie nodded. 'Just . . . be careful. Promise.'

The key turned in the lock and the door swung

open, filling the air with the stench of acrid smoke and burnt skin.

'*Tick-tock*,' came the voice, not remotely human any more.

'Now!' Ru yelled. Before Cribbins could move, Malik and Elfie flew past him and out through the door.

With a pounding heart, Ru darted to the jumble of flowers, but before she could escape, Cribbins snarled and hurled himself at the door. He jammed the key in the lock, panting like a wounded animal.

No. Ru froze. *I'm trapped.*

Through the blood and bruises, his eyes glinted red. His uniform was in tatters, and he was almost wolf-like, with clawed fingers and shredded lips baring sharp, broken teeth. At his feet, flames blazed, and ash scattered from his shoes as he strode down the aisle towards her.

'The others don't matter anyway,' he growled. 'You're the only one I really need, Ruby Cole.'

Elfie's screams and fists pounded at the door. 'No! Ru!'

'Get going, Elfie!' Ru yelled, keeping her eyes locked on the creature in front of her. Smiling like a gargoyle, he crept towards her with sparks of fire.

'Ru, I'm not gonna leave...'

'Go! Malik needs you!' Ru shouted. She lifted her foot and summoned up all the feelings she'd locked away for months – anger, fear, hatred – and then stamped it, hard. The bluebells and hawthorns snapped and ground beneath her trainers.

Cribbins staggered back and fell on to the floor, letting out a blood-curdling scream.

'You're going to listen to me now, Cribbins.' Triumphantly, she watched him squirm on the carpet. 'I know why you want me in here the most. It's because of Syd Cole, the driver of this train. My ancestor. Yeah, I know your plan. Never underestimate a Wiltshire girl.'

THIRTY-THREE

Cribbins twitched violently and peered through the fingers covering his face. Blisters formed on the small amount of surviving skin.

'His fault,' he spat. 'Sydney Cole.'

Out the window, the eerie shape of Glastonbury Tor burnt through the smoke. The viaduct was near. But she couldn't think about that now.

'You hated Syd even before this. Why? You grew up together in Melbridge. Shouldn't that mean something?'

'Lazy... feckless... stupid...'

'You're wrong,' Ru cut him off. 'Disorganized, yes. Messy, yes. That's a family trait. But that doesn't make someone lazy, or stupid. Order can be pretty awesome – believe me, I know – but it's not the only way. You didn't trust him, but the crash wasn't his fault, Cribbins.'

'Selfish ... killed us all ...'

Ru stamped on the flowers again, and Cribbins cowered, whimpering.

The long blur of the viaduct loomed, and her stomach flipped. Trees hid beneath the arches like frightened insects. How could anything be so impossibly high? The train jolted and stumbled, not slowing, but getting faster.

Come on, Syd.

'Syd Cole didn't cause the accident. He did the best that he could. The wind knocked the signal and he didn't know he was supposed to slow down. He still managed to brake on time, but the coupling was loose on the coal carriage. Just two small bits of bad luck that added up to an unbelievable tragedy. But he was *not* to blame.'

Overcome with bravery – or was it stupidity? – Ru stepped away from the flowers and knelt cautiously by Cribbins' side. 'It wasn't fair. You deserved a family, and a career, and a life. It sucked that you didn't get one. I'm sorry.'

Cribbins took his hands from his ruined face. Ru's

muscles tightened, but the eyes that stared back at her weren't the same. They were sad. Desperately sad.

There was a deafening screech of metal. The brakes: louder than the wail of fireworks, louder than a thousand nails on a thousand blackboards, and Ru knew the end was coming.

She sank to the floor and wrapped herself in a hug, praying that it would be quick, that she wouldn't know anything about it, and that it would be the same for Elfie too, and that Malik wouldn't take it too hard because he tried his best, and...

There was an almighty heave backwards. Cabinet doors flew open, the suitcases fell like rain, and Ru went flying, Cribbins flung in the opposite direction. She landed on her stomach and braced for the sensation of the fall. For the landing.

THIRTY-FOUR

But none came.

Only a deathly silence.

Was she dead?

There was a curse, and a groan.

Heart hammering, Ru pulled herself up to standing and peered over the top of the armchair.

Had Malik managed to tell Syd? Had he stopped in time?

A dust-covered figure climbed off the floor and patted down his creased uniform. He grabbed his hat, which appeared to have rolled underneath a neighbouring table, smoothed his hair, placed it on his head and turned to face the carriage.

'Miss?' he said, clearly shocked to see her. 'Are you quite all right?'

Ru gaped at him. Apart from the slight cut at the corner of his eye, he looked exactly like he had when she'd first crossed his path. Pristine, youthful, with piercing blue eyes and an open expression.

'I . . .' she gulped.

They'd done it. Malik and Syd had done it. She was so relieved she almost blacked out.

He stared at her. 'I'm so sorry, I don't believe we've met. Are you from Melbridge? How did . . . ?' He tilted his head and narrowed his eyes. 'That is, we *have* met, haven't we?'

'It was a long time ago,' Ru managed at last. 'Don't worry if you've forgotten.'

'Well, that was a rather close shave,' he announced, sliding the window open. 'We almost headed up the viaduct at full speed.' A strong gust of smoky wind poured into the carriage. 'No guessing who was to blame for that.'

'I think . . .' Ru managed. 'That is, I hear there was a problem with the signal, and a coupling system broke. But the driver somehow managed to stop before we reached the viaduct. No harm done.'

'He did?' Cribbins frowned. 'Syd Cole did that?'

'Mm-hmm.'

A pause, and Cribbins broke into a disbelieving chuckle. 'Well, I'll be . . . Good on you, Syd. Good on you.'

He smiled at Ru and pulled the watch from his pocket.

Ru couldn't hear any ticking at all.

'5.07.' He clicked his tongue on his teeth. 'We'd better hurry up if we want to catch the sunrise. I'll get everyone off the train. We can walk the rest of the way.' He unlocked the door and held it open, gesturing for Ru to pass. 'Come along. Tick-tock.'

Ru drank in her freedom like water. No sooner had she stepped off the train than she was greeted with a blur of mermaid colour and a bear hug.

'He did it!' Elfie screamed in her ear. 'He warned Syd! He saved the train!'

A family stepped off *The Green Lady* and on to the grass. A man, a woman and two children were all dressed for May Day celebrations, wearing green, old-fashioned costumes and their faces painted with multi-coloured symbols. Antlers wrapped in ivy vines were glued on to the man's tweed hat, and the little girl was clutching something tightly to her chest.

It was the broken doll Ru had seen in the Melbridge museum.

The back of her eyes began to sting.

'Malik should see all the lives he saved. Where is he?'

'Over there.' A little sadly, Elfie pointed up the platform, to a dirt-covered boy wearing a two-tone cat as a scarf. 'Ru, he didn't know who I was.'

Malik was mid-conversation with two men in overalls. One of them, despite being slick with sweat, had frizzy red hair that bounced from his head like a fireball. The other had a cleft in his chin. They both glared at the coupling hook in shock, then patted Malik on the shoulder and ruffled his hair. The boy beamed with pride and tickled Ned's fur. Then he turned around and stared directly at Ru and Elfie.

'Wait. Does he . . . ?'

'I don't know.'

Malik considered them for a few moments, before cautiously raising his hand in half a wave. Then his face went blank, and he vanished into the crowd.

'Bye, Malik,' Ru said, waving back. The tears blurred his small frame. 'I hope you have a good life.'

'Sydney?' A familiar voice called behind them,

and heavy footsteps sank into the dew-soaked grass.

Standing beside the cab, Syd looked up, his eyes darkening. 'Jim,' he growled, in the same Wiltshire lilt as Gram.

Ru's stomach sank.

Cribbins hastened to Syd, the keys jangling at his side. Ru couldn't hear what was said, but she saw Cribbins remove his hat and extend his hand. She saw Syd gaze at it in confusion, then take it with his own big, coal-smudged palm, and grin in surprise.

THIRTY-FIVE

They took a seat at the top of the Tor so they could watch the May Day festivities. The wind had dropped, and the sun was rising rapidly. It warmed their tired bones.

'When do they do it?' Ru asked Elfie, whose outline glowed pink with the early light.

'When the sun rises. Any second now.' Elfie pulled Ru to her feet. 'Look, there it goes.'

'Oh, *wow*!'

One by one, stretching far beyond the horizon, specks of orange flame materialized in a line. It was like fireflies dancing in the dawn. 'The Michael Line beacons,' Elfie said, awestruck. 'Lit along the sun's path. Celebrating the beginning of summer.'

The future seemed suddenly full of light. For Ru,

too. The prickly porcupine that had curled up around her heart had vanished. She didn't know what was going to happen with her family. But maybe that was OK. Towards the end, everything good had gone, anyway – replaced with cross words and slammed doors – and it was only after the split she'd seen either of her parents smile again. It was like they'd shed their skin. New chances were like that.

It hurt right now. But it wouldn't hurt forever. And summer was coming.

The Glastonbury Tor beacon roared alight. Ru threw her head back and let her old life fade into the darkness.

'I welcome in the new light!' she yelled to the dawn. 'You hear me? Whatever it brings!'

A swift called back with the scream of its whistle, and Ru watched it weave through the bonfire smoke and disappear into the clouds.

Morris dancers shook their bells and banged their sticks of hazel. Far above them, Elfie copied their movements like a secret shadow. 'See? I think I'll join a troupe.'

Cream cakes and strawberries and flasks of hot tea were scoffed on picnic blankets. Children twisted coloured ribbons round a maypole, and to Ru's delight, a familiar girl was one of them, and she held a familiar doll tightly in her spare hand. The doll had a ribbon in her hair now.

A giant green figure wearing antlers was paraded on shoulders. The figure was draped with an elegant cloak of leaves trimmed with fresh yellow flowers.

'The Green Man,' Elfie said wistfully. 'Here to protect us all.'

'Just like him.' Ru nodded to the shape of the boy chasing the cat around a tree, illuminated by the sun. 'Do you think he'll remember anything?'

'I hope not,' said Elfie. Ru burrowed her head into Elfie's neck, calmed by the scent of cherries, and listened to the melody floating up the Tor. Strains of a violin and faraway singers, were carried by the breeze.

So, Hail! Hail! The First of May-o!
For it is the first summer's day-o!
Cast your cares and fears away,
Drink to the Green Man on the First of May . . . !

But when Ru lifted her head from Elfie's, the musicians had vanished. And so had everybody else.

The Tor was completely empty.

'Elfie, look...'

A strange buzz came from Ru's pocket. She ignored it and shifted her weight slightly. It came again, and again, and irritated her thigh. The same buzz came from Elfie's pocket, too.

'Oh my days,' Elfie squeaked. 'It's our phones.'

'It's not?!' Heart in her mouth, Ru grabbed at hers. All the power. All the bars. Full signal. And message after message was pouring in.

Checking in

Where are u

U ok

Ru this isnt funny

Are u dead

Answer yr fone

Telling mum

Told mum

Told dad

You have a new voicemail

You have a new voicemail

You have a new voicemail

'Ooft.' Ru held it at arm's length, like it was about to explode. 'They're going to kill me.'

The phone buzzed again, vibrating so violently that it almost fell from her hand and tumbled down the Tor. Somebody was calling her.

She pressed answer without even checking the name.

'*Ruby?*' came the frantic voice at the other end. '*RU, IS THAT YOU?*'

'It's me,' she croaked. 'Hi, Mum.'

'*GWYN, SHE'S ANSWERED! Oh my god, where are you, baby?*'

'Ha... funny story...' She laughed weakly. By the sounds of it, Elfie was having the exact same call as her. 'I'm on top of Glastonbury Tor. Um... can you come get me?'

Thirty-six

A few hours later they were all bundled into Gram's kitchen, gobbling steamed apple porridge and homemade honey cake. For some inexplicable reason, Ru was *starving*.

Elfie's parents were on their way from Ogbourne, heading to Melbridge for an early morning breakfast. Once their families had cried, and shouted, and established they were safe and unhurt, they'd promised to leave questions until after a big sleep. So they still had a few hours to figure all that out.

'May Day honey cake,' Gram said, peering at Ru owlishly. 'You two deserve a bit of sweetness. Tricksters and ghosts abound on May Eve, isn't that right? Especially on ley lines beneath a blood moon.'

'Still on about all that, Clara?' Dad planted a kiss on her cheek and swiped a slice of cake from her hand. 'Box of frogs, this one.'

As she always had, Gram chuckled at him fondly and thwacked him with a tea towel. 'Just can't get rid of you, can we Gwyn?'

'Not a chance.' Dad stopped at Ru's chair and held out his arms. Mum slid beneath one, and grumbling, Sam edged into the other.

'Because we're a family,' Mum said, and Ru felt her hand squeeze her shoulder. 'Married or not, that won't change. The Cole-Darkes may be messy and imperfect, but we stick together. Whatever that looks like from now on.'

'All right,' Sam grunted. 'Cringe.'

Ru felt another hand on her shoulder. Dad's. The lump in her stomach she'd felt since the split had formed into a new shape. It still hurt and weighed heavily. But it didn't feel deadly any more. And maybe one day it would get lighter.

'Here's to messy and imperfect,' Dad announced, holding his honey cake in the air.

'Messy and imperfect!' they chanted to the chorus of clinking mugs.

The kitchen clock chimed with eight bells. Somehow it was 8 a.m., and the longest night Ru had ever known was over.

Gram sighed and unhooked her pinny. 'Only three hours until we open. Suppose I'd better get some sleep.'

'Do you have to be on today, Ma?' Mum yawned. 'Can't one of the neighbours do it?'

'Until what opens?' Ru's ears pricked up. She lowered the cake before it could reach her mouth. 'What neighbours?'

The grown-ups exchanged a look.

'Rubes, maybe you should get some sleep, too,' Dad said gently.

'Why, Melbridge Steamworks, Firecrest.' Gram looked nonplussed. 'The vintage train centre we open to the public. Co-owned by all of us in the railway cottages, remember?'

'I . . .' Ru felt like a firework was about to go off in her head. 'Course I do. Hey, can I just show Elfie round while it's empty – really quickly?'

'I don't think . . .' frowned Mum.

'We won't wander off, I promise. And we'll only be a couple of minutes.' Ru was already slipping on her trainers, shooting wide, obviously-secret-code eyes to Elfie.

'I love trains!' Elfie bounded off her chair so quickly that it fell backwards. 'I'd love to. Got my camera, y'know...' She waved it weakly.

'I'm happy to take them down for a minute, Martha.' Gram joined them at the door. 'Couple of things I've got to do before sleep anyway.'

'Well, if you're sure...' Mum still looked doubtful, but Dad swiftly took the empty mug from her hand.

'Off you trot,' he said. 'You deserve a rest. I'll knock you up a camomile tea before I go.'

Before anyone could change their mind, Ru flung the door open and darted outside. Now the sun rose over the Wiltshire hills, she saw dozens of railway cottages in gleaming limestone, lined up in proud rows. Summer flower pots decorated porches, rose bushes towered over fences, curtains glowed with inside lights. Dogs barked. Milk bottles clinked. Even Gram's gnome still had his head on.

No place like gnome.

'Oh...' she whispered. 'Melbridge is *alive*.' She breathed out, letting go of all the bad memories and the stuff that didn't exist any more. Her puff made steam swirls in the sunshine.

Elfie sidled up to her, nose wrinkled in confusion. 'So, what's up?'

'They were all in ruins. *Before*,' Ru whispered, keenly aware of Gram pottering about on the driveway. 'Most of them had been knocked down.'

Elfie's eyes widened. 'You're joking.'

'Firecrest? Want to take your friend down there?'

Ru followed Gram's eyeline to the bottom of the valley. There, filling the space where the broken sheds, the vine-drowned ticket office and the littered tracks had once been, was a mass of smart buildings in brown stone. Steam trains rested inside the Engine Shed. EDUCATION CENTRE was on one door. THE STATION CAFÉ on another. MELBRIDGE STEAMWORKS was proudly emblazoned on a vintage sign that hung over a whitewashed platform, dotted with plant beds and hanging baskets. TICKET OFFICE MUSEUM was etched into the platform door.

She careered down the path with Elfie at her side, crossing the tracks and leaping on to the platform.

'Hold your horses.' Gram shuffled up behind

them, holding a key out in front of her. 'Some of us don't have your young bones.' She unlocked the door and switched on the light. 'You've got two minutes. I'm just popping to switch the coffee machines on. We don't want the costumed volunteers to go on strike.'

Ru barely heard her. Mouth agape, she wandered into the museum, taking in the gleaming exhibition cases, the old uniforms on display and the enormous canvas pictures of MWL employees covering the walls. They were laughing in the Engine Shed. Grouped in front of a train in pinafores and hats. Dancing in green costumes on Glastonbury Tor.

'Malik Marley,' she whispered. 'You did more than save a train. You saved a whole world.'

THIRTY-SEVEN

'Hey Ru,' Elfie called softly. 'There's something that *you* can take credit for. Look.' She tapped the display case in front of her.

Ru went to Elfie's side, staying close. Her mouth was as dry as a bone. Inside the display case was a pristine 1920s uniform. A hat bearing the *MWL* insignia. A ticket punch. A pocket watch.

And on the wall next to it was a framed photograph of a moustachioed old man, mid-dance step and wearing a joyous, goofy grin.

JIM CRIBBINS RETIREMENT, 1972.

Two men had their arms linked through his. One about the same age, with wiry white hair that exploded from his head. And another, much shorter, and about ten years younger, with greying hair.

'Jim Cribbins was friends with your great-great-grampy.' Gram appeared at her shoulder. 'The longest-serving conductor on the Mid Wessex Line. He loved that job, he did. And the passengers all loved him.'

Elfie reached for Ru's hand. 'They did? Why?'

'Ah,' smiled Gram. 'He was one of the best. A more decent, kinder chap you'd be hard pressed to find. Not always, mind. Some said he'd started out a grumpy so-and-so, but there was a near miss with a train accident in 1925, and it changed him. He always said it made him see things in a new light. Gave him a second chance, you know.'

'And . . .' Ru's finger went to the short man at his side. 'Who's that?'

'Oh, bless him,' Gram said fondly. 'That was Malik Marley.'

Ru's heart thudded painfully. 'Was?'

'He died last year. 109, can you believe it? And he was still driving trains until he was 101.'

'Of course he was.' Salty tears streamed down Ru's cheeks. 'Of course.'

Gram yawned, plonked the keys in Elfie's palm

and shuffled towards the door. 'Right, I'm off to bed. I need at least two hours sleep before I drive a train. Turn the light off and lock up once you're done, will you?' She blew a kiss and disappeared on to the platform.

'Will do,' Ru called, despite the fact she didn't know how to do either.

'Hey, Ru...' Elfie said. 'There's something behind the picture frame.'

Ru squinted. A tiny white triangle was poking out at the corner. She pulled at it, and a creased envelope slid out. *Ruby and Elfleda* was printed on a faded label.

'What? How...?' Ru stared at it in amazement. Hands clammy, she tore it open.

'Careful,' Elfie winced. 'It could be old.'

The paper *was* a little fragile, but it wasn't that old at all. It was written in blue biro, with the date *3 April 2013* at the top.

'That's my birthday,' Ru whispered. 'I mean – the day I was born.'

'Shall I read it out?' said Elfie. 'Your eyes look too puffy.'

'Yes please.'

'Dear Ru and Elfie,

I expect this is a shock, especially as you saw me just a few hours ago.

It took me a long time to remember. Mostly it came to me in dreams, or brief flashes of memories I didn't understand. For a while I was obsessed with bluebells. And then this morning, Clara – your grandmother, Ru – told me that Martha had given birth to a daughter, Ruby. And like a light had been switched on, everything came back. How you helped me save the train.

I just wanted to tell you that I have – had, most likely, by the time you read this – a good life. I have been happy. I have been a train driver for seventy or so years, although now I'm confined to short tourist lines rather than cross-country. I married the love of my life, Ivy. We had two beautiful daughters. Their middle names are Ruby and Elfleda, although I didn't know why then. I fought in the war, like so many others, but unlike them, I came home. Despite the shrapnel in my elbow, I was lucky. I always have been, it seems.

Station Ned lived for ten more years, ate a lot of chicken and went on many train rides all over the country. He died peacefully at home, and is buried under a rose bush. Perhaps it's still there. Do say hello if so.

Jim Cribbins was much changed. I don't know how much he remembered, although sometimes I'd see him looking at me oddly, but we never discussed it. He was a good person, eventually. He was my friend.

Allow me, as an old man, to reinforce the wisdom you once shared with me, Ru. Some things you can control, others you can't. Choose wisely, and let the rest go.

Your friend forever, in thanks and remembrance,
Malik Marley.'

Loved this? Read on for chapter one of
THE WITCHSTONE GHOSTS
by Emily Randall-Jones...

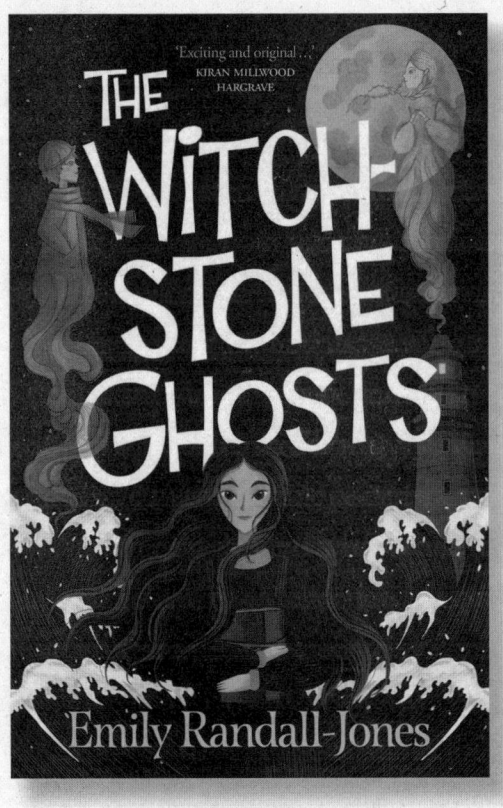

AVAILABLE NOW!

1

If I'm honest, Autumn thought, *I'd quite like to be the same as everybody else.*

She was standing on an underground tube station platform with a gentleman in a top hat on one side of her and a woman in overalls on the other. They were talking at the same time, because both were competing for her attention.

Anyone alive watching Autumn would've seen a small twelve-year-old girl with large, sea-tinted eyes and wild dark curls stuffed under a mustard bobble hat. Anyone alive would have assumed Autumn was absorbed in her book, when in fact she'd read the same sentence forty-three times because Overalls Ghost was singing Second World War songs in her ear and Top Hat Ghost was moaning about King Edward VII.

A guttural roar and a flash of lights and the tube train rumbled through the tunnel. The carriage doors swept open with a *beep* and Autumn dashed nimbly inside, squeezing herself into a corner. The ghosts, unable to leave the station, chased the train the length of the platform as it departed, *swooshing* through waiting commuters and stone pillars until they stopped dead at an advert for skin cream.

Phew. There were too many passengers squashed together with bulky coats and bags for a ghost to reach her here. She briefly considered just going round on the tube all day instead of going to school, but they'd call Mum – again – and she'd have to make up a reason – again – and quite frankly it was easier to just show up and hope nobody noticed her.

The tube juddered. Stuffing the decoy book back into her school bag, Autumn pulled out a pen and brown notebook and scribbled as best she could without fully extending her elbows.

ARCHWAY TUBE STATION, SOUTHBOUND PLATFORM
- Overalls Ghost
- Top Hat Ghost

She decided to omit 'both told me to beware' because recently ghosts had loved telling her to beware. It was one of their things and hardly worth noting any more.

In the past six months she'd had to stop walking to school because of Wailing Park Ghost, stop getting the bus because of Conductor Ghost that kept asking for her ticket, and use a different tube station because Christian the Tufnell Park Ghost had been particularly noisy about the upcoming apocalypse. Granted, he was one of her usuals. But he'd been a lot chattier recently.

But it wouldn't get to her today. Today was special. She would go through anything to get to that evening, because *finally* Dad was coming home.

He'd been leading the West Country birding tours for over a month now. He'd never ventured as far as Devon or Cornwall before, and even though he'd stopped by a phone box once a week or so (Mum thought mobile phones sent information to the government and had banned them) – 'Wrynecks today, it's migration time!', 'Went to a pub with a well for a table!' – they'd not heard much and she missed the very bones of him. Tonight they were cycling to Hampstead Heath to spot barn owls by moonlight and eat sandwiches under the stars.

Dad was coming home.

She hugged that thought to her chest like a hot-water bottle.

AUTHOR NOTE

I have taken some artistic license (ahem) with some of the railway stations and the semaphore signalling design. Several stations in this book are fictional and there's no viaduct above Glastonbury Tor – it was inspired by Dundas Aqueduct. Melbridge and the Mid Wessex Line were based on Swindon Steamworks and the Great Western Railway. My own Great-Grandpa, Syd Taylor, worked at the Steamworks until a suspended train collapsed on him and he lost his leg. He was put on medical retirement and spent his remaining years as the beloved caretaker at a Swindon primary school. Taylor Crescent in Stratton St. Margaret is named after him.

My other Great-Grandpa, Gomer Thomas, was Station Master at Blaengwynfi, another station that no longer exists.

Signalling accidents did happen, and in 1876 a train crashed at high speed because a blizzard froze the signal arm in the 'all clear' position. However, by 1925, when the fictional *Green Lady* crashed, semaphore signals had been redesigned to avoid accidents caused by signal malfunctions.

In nearly every town and village in the UK, there are haunting remnants of a lost railway line or station: a long, straight path, often high up; a half-collapsed tunnel; piles of bricks, split by tree roots – nature taking everything back.

Emily Randall-Jones
March 2025

ACKNOWLEDGEMENTS

I'll try and keep this shorter than the last one. I'll probably fail, because I'm constantly supported by a million brilliant people, and I tend to babble. I'm also going to say a blanket I'm-sorry-if-I've-missed-anyone-out statement now. I love you, I'm just mega forgetful.

Thank you to this lovely lot:

Rachel L – phenomenal editor/person. Thank you for taking a messy lump of a first draft and shaping it into the folksy spookathon it was always meant to be. Everything is down to you! (Also sorry about the midnight emails about ideas I had in a dream.)

The Chicken House Wonder Coop: Barry, Laura, Elinor, Rachel H, Shalu, Esther, Ruth and Emily – it's such an honour to be part of the team. Thank you for all your phenomenal work, and for the many cakes and biscuits I've enjoyed in your company.

Micaela Alcaino, for another stunning cover. I love how my book babies look next to each other.

Dave Webber – cannot thank you enough for letting me use your wonderful folk song 'Hail! Hail, the First of May! (May Song)'. Listen to it for the authentic Green Lady experience...

My agent Lucy, for guiding my career so thoughtfully, and for listening to my many, many half-formed ideas that I will inevitably forget, and gently reminding me of the right ones. Hope you enjoy the sneaky *Doctor Who* references.

Everyone at WriteMentor – Stuart, Melissa and Florianne and all of the Hub writers I've had the pleasure of working with. Special mention to the Neurodivergent Writers' Group. I love our brains and our safe space.

The Society of Authors for supporting this project with a grant, which gave me extra time and space to write. An absolute lifesaver.

There are so many brilliant book bloggers, booksellers, teachers and librarians who championed *The Witchstone Ghosts* and I'm so sorry if I don't list everyone, but it's meant the world. Special mention to Hannah and Becky at Mr B's Emporium, Emma and Rachel at Canterbury Waterstones, Ann Stokes at St John's School, Marlborough (hope you spot your name in the story!) Jonathon Douglass and the teachers and students of Christchurch,

Bradford-on-Avon, and the teams behind the Brilliant Book Award, the Stockton Children's Book of the Year and the Phoenix Book Award. I'm constantly amazed at the love and passion that you all bring.

Bathstol Writerz, Kidlit Chin Waggers, Team Irvine and Chickens – sorry I'm rubbish at answering messages and going to book launches.

Brilliant writerly friends who are brilliant at both writing and being a friend through everything. Marisa Linton, Laura Caputo-Wickham, Sanam Akram, Sara Lilley, Gillian Bentley-Richardson, Lucille Abendanon, Carey Camburn, Gavin Tangen, Clare Harlow, Phililp Kavvadias, Alex Atkinson, Amy Feest, Cate Haynes, Stephen Daly, Thomas Leeds (and his excellent parents), and Marnie Forbes-Eldridge.

My friends who aren't writers but are still brilliant: NCT mums – special shout out to Gemma Teale and Lisa O'Brien, Miranda Lot – particular mention to Caitriona Horne and Frankie Edwards of the publishing/old flatmates Venn diagram for guesting on WM, Ed Thomas and the kittens, Sophie and Ed Kerr and Perrie Dunnett.

Nearly done, I promise...

My Stars Hollow-esque town, for welcoming me and my babies two years ago and giving us the most wonderful community. Particular mention to Helly and Sophia Borne, Rachael Scotson, Clare Hobbs, Sarah McGain and all the brilliant parents who watch my kids so I can write/sleep, Angie at Mercy in Action for telling me to stop procrastinating and write, Little Rituals for the iced lattes, Shambles Nursery, Day Lewis for keeping me in Elvanse during the shortage, and the Steward family for lending me their daughter's beautiful name.

Pete, for being the Gwyn to my Martha and co-smashing this co-parenting thing.

My Great-Aunt, Jennifer Lever, who sadly passed away recently. The possessor of an incredible mind, a love of folk music and books, and a thirst for knowledge that was unmatched. You deserve to be remembered and celebrated.

Mum, Dad and my sister Lu. Thanks for dressing up as *Ghosts* characters on my birthday. Love you all to bits. Daisy and Bertie, for being utterly magical and for surprising me every day. I love you more than books and cups of tea.

And finally, to all the young people and their parents who are going through the painful process of separation. You're not alone, even though you might feel it sometimes. It hurts right now, but it won't always, I promise. And summer is coming.

We are grateful for permission from the author to reproduce adapted extracts from 'Hail! Hail! The First of May-o/May Song', original lyrics by Dave Webber, © Dave Webber 1990.